CORPUS SIGNORUM IMPERII ROMANI
CORPUS OF SCULPTURE OF THE ROMAN WORLD

THE BRITISH ACADEMY

CORPUS SIGNORUM IMPERII ROMANI
CORPUS OF SCULPTURE OF THE ROMAN WORLD

GREAT BRITAIN

Volume I   Fascicule 4

SCOTLAND

BY

L. J. F. KEPPIE

AND

BEVERLY J. ARNOLD

PUBLISHED FOR THE BRITISH ACADEMY
BY THE OXFORD UNIVERSITY PRESS

Oxford University Press, Walton Street, Oxford OX2 6DP
London New York Toronto
Delhi Bombay Calcutta Madras Karachi
Kuala Lumpur Singapore Hong Kong Tokyo
Nairobi Dar es Salaam Cape Town
Melbourne Auckland
and associate companies in
Beirut Berlin Ibadan Mexico City Nicosia

Oxford is a trade mark of Oxford University Press

Published in the United States by Oxford University Press, New York

British Library Cataloguing in Publication Data
Corpus signorum imperii Romani = Corpus of
sculpture of the Roman world.
Vol. 1. Fasc. 4: Scotland
1. Sculpture, Roman—Catalogs
I. Keppie, L. J. F.   II. Arnold, Beverly
II. British Academy
733'.5'0216   NB115
ISBN 0-19-726026-8

Printed in Great Britain
at the University Press, Oxford
by David Stanford
Printer to the University

CONTENTS

PREFACE

BRITAIN's contribution to the international Corpus of Sculpture of the Roman World (*Corpus Signorum Imperii Romani*) is being published in three volumes, each consisting of a series of fascicules. The first volume, which is under the aegis of the British Academy, covers sculpture from Roman Britain, the second and third volumes Roman sculpture from abroad which has reached Britain in comparatively recent times.

Dr Keppie's fascicule is the fourth in Volume I. The first was *Corbridge, Hadrian's Wall East of the North Tyne*, by E. J. Phillips (1977), the second *Bath and the rest of Wessex*, by B. W. Cunliffe and M. Fulford (1982), and the third *Yorkshire* by S. Rinaldi Tufi (1983). Work on the fifth fascicule, on *Wales*, by Mr R. J. Brewer, is nearing completion, and another, on *Hadrian's Wall West of the North Tyne*, was in an advanced state of preparation by Mr E. J. Phillips, when illness compelled him to retire from academic work. The committee wishes to place on record its deep gratitude to Mr Phillips for his major contribution to the Corpus.

As each fascicule appears, so the regional characteristics and diversity of sculpture in Roman Britain become more apparent. It remains to express the committee's thanks both to Dr Keppie for his meticulous study of the material in Scotland and, for the planning of the plates, to Mr Nick Clarke.

Newcastle upon Tyne
31 May 1984

R. M. HARRISON
Secretary to the National Committee

ACKNOWLEDGEMENTS

THE production of this fascicule was financed by the British Academy, and written under the supervision of the British Committee of *CSIR*; we are grateful for the trust and support of both bodies. The task of writing the Scottish fascicule was originally undertaken by Professor Anne S. Robertson, but was transferred to Lawrence Keppie as one of his first responsibilities on taking up an appointment at the Hunterian Museum in 1973. The pressure of other commitments impeded progress. However, in 1980, when he was joined by Beverly Arnold as co-editor, the impetus quickened, and the fascicule reached its final form in the autumn of 1982.

A substantial part of the initial indexing of stones was done in 1972 by Miss Dorcas Pajakovska-Dydynska (now Mrs Thomas), under Professor Robertson's supervision, and (for the National Museum of Antiquities) by Dr D. V. Clarke: we wish to thank them for laying so carefully the groundwork for the fascicule. Professor R. M. Harrison, secretary of the British committee of *CSIR*, willingly offered his support and advice throughout its compilation.

We are also delighted to record our thanks to the directors and staffs of the Hunterian Museum, Glasgow Art Gallery and Museum, The National Museum of Antiquities of Scotland, Dundee Art Gallery and Museum, Dumfries Museum, Falkirk Museum, and the Scottish Development Department (Ancient Monuments), for permission to examine and measure stones in their care, for providing an extensive range of excellent photographs, and for the permission to reproduce some of them here.

The photographs of nos. 53, 72, 82, and 128 were taken by Dr L. Keppie; Dr V. A. Maxfield kindly provided a photograph of no. 164. The Royal Commission on the Ancient and Historical Monuments of Scotland supplied a photograph of no. 65 and gave permission for it to be reproduced. The line-drawing of no. 26 was prepared by John Callan, of no. 27 by Avril Mackenzie, and of no. 135 by the late Margaret Scott. The photographs of nos. 95 and 101 were made available by the British Library; line-drawings of stones now lost were photographed from the antiquarian writers by Glasgow University's Photographic Unit.

The final typescript was read through in its entirety by Mr R. Goodburn and Dr D. J. Breeze, and we have benefited considerably from their advice and suggestions, many of which are gratefully incorporated.

Many individuals helped with locating and interpreting the pieces discussed, and particular mention should be made of our debt to Mr T. Cowie and Mr I. Scott (National Museum of Antiquities), Dr T. F. C. Blagg, Mr M. W. C. Hassall, Mr N. McQ. Holmes, Mr G. S. Maxwell, Dr E. A. Cormack, Mrs P. Maxwell-Scott, Mr H. B. Millar, Mr W. N. Robertson, and Dr Susan Wilkes.

Hunterian Museum
University of Glasgow
31 July 1983

L. J. F. KEPPIE
BEVERLY J. ARNOLD

BIBLIOGRAPHY

Anderson 1896	J. Anderson, 'The Pottery, Bronze, etc., found at Birrens', *PSAS* xxx, 1895-6, pp. 179-99
Anderson 1898	J. Anderson, 'Notices of the Pottery, Bronze and other Articles discovered during the excavations' [at Ardoch], *PSAS* xxxii, 1897-8, pp. 453-71
Anderson 1901	J. Anderson, 'Notices of the Pottery, Bronze and other Objects found at Camelon', *PSAS* xxxv, 1900-1, pp. 380-417
Anderson 1905	J. Anderson, 'Notice of the Pottery, Bronze and other Articles found at Rough Castle', *PSAS* xxxix, 1904-5, pp. 489-97
Clarke 1933	J. Clarke, *The Roman Fort at Cadder*, Glasgow, 1933
Clarke, Breeze, and Mackay 1980	D. V. Clarke, D. J. Breeze, and G. Mackay, *The Romans in Scotland*, Edinburgh, 1980
Curle 1911	J. Curle, *A Roman Frontier Post and its People: the Fort of Newstead in the Parish of Melrose*, Glasgow, 1911
Espérandieu	É. Espérandieu, *Recueil général des bas-reliefs, statues et bustes de la Gaule romaine*, Paris, 1907-66
Gordon 1726	A. Gordon, *Itinerarium Septentrionale*, London, 1726
Gordon 1732	A. Gordon, *Additions and Corrections, by Way of Supplement to the Itinerarium Septentrionale*, London, 1732
Gough 1806	W. Camden, *Britannia*, ed. by R. Gough, London, 1806
Hodgson 1840	J. Hodgson, *A History of Northumberland*, part ii, vol. iii, Newcastle, 1840
Horsley 1732	J. Horsley, *Britannia Romana*, London, 1732
Keppie 1979	L. Keppie, *Roman Distance Slabs from the Antonine Wall*, Glasgow, 1979
Laskey 1813	J. Laskey, *A General Account of the Hunterian Museum, Glasgow*, Glasgow, 1813
McCaul 1863	J. McCaul, *Britanno-Roman Inscriptions*, Toronto, 1863
Macdonald 1934	G. Macdonald, *The Roman Wall in Scotland*, edn. 2, Oxford, 1934
Macdonald and Park 1906	G. Macdonald and A. Park, *The Roman Forts on the Bar Hill*, Glasgow, 1906
Macdonald and Curle 1929	G. Macdonald and A. O. Curle, 'The Roman Fort at Mumrills, near Falkirk', *PSAS* lxiii, 1928-9, pp. 396-575
Macdonald 1896	J. Macdonald, 'Account of the Excavations at Birrens . . . The Inscribed Stones', *PSAS* xxx, 1895-6, pp. 121-69
Macdonald 1897	J. Macdonald, *Tituli Hunteriani: an Account of the Roman Stones in the Hunterian Museum, University of Glasgow*, Glasgow, 1897
Macdonald and Barbour 1897	J. Macdonald and J. Barbour, *Birrens and its Antiquities*, Dumfries, 1897
Maitland 1757	W. Maitland, *History and Antiquities of Scotland*, London, 1757
Miller 1922	S. N. Miller, *The Roman Fort at Balmuildy*, Glasgow, 1922
Nichols 1790	J. Nichols (ed.), *Bibliotheca Topographica Britannica*, vol. iii, London, 1790
Pennant 1776	T. Pennant, *A Tour in Scotland and Voyage to the Hebrides MDCCLXXII*, Chester and London, 1774-6

Phillips 1977   E. J. Phillips, *Corpus Signorum Imperii Romani: Great Britain*, vol. i, fasc. i: *Corbridge, Hadrian's Wall east of the North Tyne*, Oxford, 1977

RCAHMS 1920   *Inventory of Monuments and Constructions in the County of Dumfries*, Edinburgh, 1920

RCAHMS 1929   *Inventory of Monuments and Constructions in the Counties of Midlothian and West Lothian*, Edinburgh, 1929

RCAHMS 1956   *An Inventory of the Ancient and Historical Monuments of Roxburghshire*, Edinburgh, 1956

RCAHMS 1963   *Stirlingshire, An Inventory of the Ancient Monuments*, Edinburgh, 1963

RCAHMS 1967   *Peeblesshire, An Inventory of the Ancient Monuments*, Edinburgh, 1967

RCAHMS 1978   *Lanarkshire, An Inventory of the Prehistoric and Roman Monuments*, Edinburgh, 1978

Robertson 1975   A. S. Robertson, *Birrens (Blatobulgium)*, Edinburgh, 1975

Robertson, Scott,   A. S. Robertson, M. Scott, and L. Keppie, *Bar Hill, A Roman Fort and its*
    and Keppie 1975   *Finds*, Oxford, 1975

Ross 1967   A. Ross, *Pagan Celtic Britain*, London, 1967

Roy 1793   W. Roy, *The Military Antiquities of the Romans in Britain*, London, 1793

Sibbald 1697   R. Sibbald, *Auctarium Musaei Balfouriani, e Musaeo Sibbaldiano . . .*, Edinburgh, 1697

Sibbald 1707   R. Sibbald, *Historical Inquiries*, Edinburgh, 1707

Stuart 1852   R. Stuart, *Caledonia Romana*, edn. 2, Edinburgh and London, 1852

Stukeley 1720   W. Stukeley, *An Account of a Roman Temple and other Antiquities, near Graham's Dike in Scotland*, London, 1720

Toynbee 1962   J. M. C. Toynbee, *Art in Roman Britain*, London, 1962

Toynbee 1964   J. M. C. Toynbee, *Art in Britain under the Romans*, Oxford, 1964

University of
    Glasgow 1768   *Monumenta Romani Imperii*, Glasgow, 1768

Wilson 1851   D. Wilson, *The Archaeology and Prehistoric Annals of Scotland*, Edinburgh, 1851

Wood 1794   J. P. Wood, *The Antient and Modern State of the Parish of Cramond*, Edinburgh, 1794

ABBREVIATIONS

AA	*Archaeologia Aeliana*
AE	*l'Année Épigraphique*
Ant. J.	*Antiquaries Journal*
Arch. J.	*Archaeological Journal*
Arch. Scot.	*Archaeologia Scotica*
BBCS	*Bulletin of the Board of Celtic Studies*
BJ	*Bonner Jahrbücher*
BM	British Museum
CIL	*Corpus Inscriptionum Latinarum*
CSIR	*Corpus Signorum Imperii Romani*
CW	*Transactions of the Cumberland & Westmorland Antiquarian and Archaeological Society*
EE	*Ephemeris Epigraphica*
Epigr. Stud.	*Epigraphische Studien*
GAJ	*Glasgow Archaeological Journal*
Gent. Mag.	*Gentleman's Magazine*
HBNC	*History of the Berwickshire Naturalists Club*
ILS	*Inscriptiones Latinae Selectae*
JRS	*Journal of Roman Studies*
MS	Manuscript
NMAS	National Museum of Antiquities of Scotland
PSA	*Proceedings of the Society of Antiquaries of London*
PSAN	*Proceedings of the Society of Antiquaries of Newcastle*
PSAS	*Proceedings of the Society of Antiquaries of Scotland*
RCAHMS	Royal Commission on the Ancient and Historical Monuments of Scotland
RE	A. Pauly-G.Wissowa, *Realencyclopädie der classischen Altertumswissenschaft*
RIB	R. G. Collingwood and R. P. Wright, *The Roman Inscriptions of Britain*, vol. i, 1965
SHR	*Scottish Historical Review*
TDGNHAS	*Transactions of the Dumfriesshire & Galloway Natural History and Antiquarian Society*
TGAS	*Transactions of the Glasgow Archaeological Society*

INTRODUCTION

Historical outline

THE earliest Roman penetration into what is now called Scotland can be dated to AD 79 or 80, when Cnaeus Julius Agricola led a major part of the provincial army northwards.[1] Agricola and his forces campaigned for five successive summers in Scotland, and penetrated at least to the Moray Firth, while his fleet circumnavigated the island. In AD 83 or 84 he won a great battle over a substantial force of Caledonians at the unidentified site of Mons Graupius.[2] Even before this victory, forts were being erected along the main lines of communication with the south, and by AD 86 construction work had begun on a fortress for the Twentieth Legion at Inchtuthil on the Tay.[3] But the transfer of troops to counter threats to other provinces nearer Rome prompted a withdrawal: by AD 90 it is likely that the Romans had already retired to the Forth–Clyde line, if not to the Cheviots, and by AD 100, or shortly after, they had completely given up all conquests north of the Tyne and Solway.

With the construction of Hadrian's Wall from 122 onwards, it must have seemed that the Roman interlude in Scotland's past was over. But with the accession of Antoninus Pius in AD 138, a fresh attempt was made to overrun southern Scotland. Political motives may have been more important than military advantage in deciding this policy.[4] The army advanced to the Forth–Clyde line and in AD 142–3 constructed across it the barrier which we know today as the Antonine Wall.[5] The new Wall was the achievement of the legions, which commemorated their contributions to its completion by setting up elaborate inscribed tablets now called 'distance slabs'.[6] The Wall was provided with forts and fortlets set at close intervals, and many other forts were built throughout southern Scotland, often on sites occupied by Agricola's forces 60 years before. A few more forts were built north of the Wall, as far as the Tay. Their purpose, evidently, was to close off, or protect, the peninsula of Fife.[7]

The occupation of Scotland in the Antonine period lasted for less than a generation. A major disaster in AD 155–7 compelled the garrisons to withdraw for a time, and many forts were burnt. Although most were soon reoccupied, it was not long before

[1] See the papers collected in *The Scottish Campaigns of Agricola*, ed. J. Kenworthy, *Scottish Archaeological Forum* xii, Edinburgh, 1981. In general, see D. J. Breeze, *The Northern Frontiers of Roman Britain* London, 1982.

[2] L. J. F. Keppie, 'Mons Graupius, the Search for a Battlefield', in J. Kenworthy (ed.), op. cit. (n. 1), pp. 79–88.

[3] L. F. Pitts, *Inchtuthil, the Roman fortress*, D.Phil. thesis, Oxford, 1982.

[4] A. R. Birley, *Transactions of the Architectural and Archaeological Society of Durham and Northumberland*, N.S. 3, 1974,

pp. 17–25.

[5] Sir G. Macdonald, *The Roman Wall in Scotland*, edn. 2, Oxford, 1934; A. S. Robertson, *The Antonine Wall*, new edn. Glasgow, 1979; W. S. Hanson and G. S. Maxwell, *Rome's North West Frontier: the Antonine Wall* Edinburgh, 1983.

[6] L. J. F. Keppie, *Roman Distance Slabs from the Antonine Wall* Glasgow, 1979.

[7] G. S. Maxwell, in *Scottish Archaeological Forum* vii, 1976, p. 42.

Scotland was finally given up, seemingly in the early 160s AD.[1] The bulk of the garrisons was withdrawn to forts on and behind Hadrian's Wall, but a few units remained beyond that frontier as far north as Newstead in the Tweed Valley. Birrens, an outpost fort for Hadrian's Wall in the west, was also retained. But both were abandoned *c*.180, and the position of the Roman frontier thereafter was little different from the Scotland–England Border with which we are familiar today.[2]

In AD 208 the emperor Septimius Severus and his sons came to Britain with large forces, and campaigned in Scotland in 209 and 210. Their forces penetrated into Aberdeenshire and perhaps beyond. In imitation of Agricola's strategy, Severus ordered the construction of a legionary base in the north, at Carpow on the south bank of the Tay, evidently seeing the value of placing a powerful force close to the most troublesome areas. Cramond fort is also known to have been reoccupied at this time. But Severus' long-term plans were not brought to fruition. He died at York early in 211. His successor Caracalla, perhaps after a final onslaught on the Caledonians in 211–12, withdrew the army to its former bases; Carpow and Cramond were abandoned.[3] Hadrian's Wall was to remain the northern frontier of Rome's British possessions for the next two centuries. Later incursions into Scotland against the Picts and other tribes were of a temporary nature, and resulted in no fresh building work.[4]

Scope of the volume

This fascicule comprises all decorative sculptured material of the Roman period known to the authors, which was found at or near known or likely Roman sites, or has a genuine provenance within the modern political boundaries of Scotland (fig. 1). The vast majority of the entries describes sculpture on stone, but the fascicule also includes a few large bronzes. Small bronze objects[5] are, in accordance with the criteria laid down for *CSIR*, excluded, and Celtic heads from non-Roman sites are not described here.[6] No attempt is made to offer a complete corpus of inscribed and sculptured material from Scotland, the former being already available to scholars in *RIB* (and its proposed Supplements), to which it is hoped that this (and other British fascicules of *CSIR*) will form a useful complement. Also excluded from this volume are sculptured slabs and bronzes surviving in country houses, museums, or private collections, which are known, or seem likely, to have been imported from England or the European continent over the last few centuries.[7] The acquisitive tendency of the Scottish baronial gentry is well known. The dividing line has been fairly clear: material probably brought into Scotland as loot in ancient times merits inclusion (e.g. nos. 45, 57), but, *inter alia*, the

[1] D. J. Breeze, in W. S. Hanson and L. J. F. Keppie (eds.), *Roman Frontier Studies 1979* Oxford, 1980, pp. 44–60.

[2] D. J. Breeze and B. Dobson, *GAJ* iv, 1976, pp. 139–40.

[3] A. R. Birley, *Septimius Severus* London, 1971, pp. 244–68; R. P. Wright, *Britannia* v, 1974, pp. 289–94.

[4] D. J. Breeze, op. cit. (p. xiii, n. 1), p. 153.

[5] See A. S. Robertson, *Britannia* i, 1970, pp. 198–226;

M. J. Green, *A Corpus of Small Cult-Objects from the military Areas of Roman Britain* Oxford, 1978.

[6] A. Ross, *Pagan Celtic Britain* London, 1967, pp. 61–126; ead., *GAJ* iii, 1974, pp. 26–33; ead., *Transactions of the Perthshire Society of Natural Science* xi, 1963–5, pp. 31–7.

[7] A. Michaelis, *Ancient Marbles in Great Britain* London, 1882, notices the most impressive collections.

fragments of a lead sarcophagus of likely Romano-British origin, now at Dumfries, which lack any evidence of Scottish provenance, have been omitted.[1]

Arrangement of entries

The entries are arranged where possible according to the geographical sequence adopted by *RIB*. In effect, therefore, there are three main sections: (1) Scotland south of the Antonine Wall; (2) sites along the frontier line itself, listed from east to west; (3) Scotland north of the Antonine Wall. The material from each site is arranged in a set sequence, following the now established order for *CSIR* fascicules: (1) representations of, or dedications to, (*a*) Graeco-Roman deities and personifications, (*b*) oriental deities, (*c*) native deities; (2) uninscribed altars; (3) funerary monuments; (4) commemorative tablets; (5) miscellaneous fragments. The whole assemblage from one site will be found together, so that some assessment is possible of the output of its garrison and the styles in vogue.

The order of presentation within each entry follows the sequence laid down for these volumes: provenance—present location—previous publication—state of preservation—measurements—technique employed—type of stone—description—comments —dating. Each surviving stone is illustrated on the accompanying numbered plates. Most of the photographs were taken especially for this project. Where stones are now lost, the illustration, if any, derives from the earliest reliable antiquarian source. At the end of the volume there is a short section of *falsa vel aliena*, briefly describing a few stones sometimes considered (wrongly in our view) to derive from Scottish sites, and a modern forgery. No account will be found of sculptures, sometimes held to be Roman by the earlier antiquarians, which modern opinion places firmly in the medieval or post-medieval period.[2] The Latin names for forts are given where the attribution seems reasonably secure; otherwise the reader is referred to A. L. F. Rivet and C. Smith, *The Place-Names of Roman Britain* (London, 1979) for further possibilities. As a result of local government reorganization in 1974, Scotland's counties ceased to exist under their old names, and a new Regional and District structure was imposed. In the following pages it has, however, seemed preferable to retain the old county designations. A large number of the stones described in the following pages have been cleaned in recent years, prior to redisplay in the National Museum of Antiquities of

---

[1] J. M. C. Toynbee, *TDGNHAS* ser. 3, xliii, 1966, pp. 80-3, with pls. vii–xi; H. Toller, *Roman Lead Coffins and Ossuaria in Britain* Oxford, 1977, no. 25.

[2] For the supposed heads of Severus and Julia Domna, once built into the Netherbow in Edinburgh, see D. Wilson, *PSAS* xix, 1884-5, pp. 203-9; for a group of four fragmentary reliefs from Perthshire showing Roman deities riding on chariots, see *RIB* 2339* and T. Ross, *PSAS* xxxvi, 1901-2, pp. 600-6 with figs.; for two cornice mouldings said to have been found on or near the fort-site at Camelon a few years before 1707, see M. Buchanan, *PSAS* xxxv, 1900-1, pp. 378-9 with figs. (Dr T. F. C. Blagg tentatively suggests a date in the eighteenth

century). Stuart (1852, pl. xiv.5) illustrates a female figure from Castlecary, carrying on her shoulder a shallow vessel. At first sight this seems to be stone, but in fact the item is a terracotta figurine, and is now preserved in the National Museum of Antiquities in Edinburgh. John Buchanan (*ap*. Stuart 1852, p. 324, n. (*a*)) also refers to 'several slender pillars with ornamented capitals, seeming to have belonged to a building, probably a small temple', found at Kirkintilloch. Their Roman origin has to remain uncertain, as the fort-site there was overlaid in part by a motte and possibly by masonry structures in the Middle Ages, all of which were long held to be remnants of the fort itself.

Scotland, Edinburgh, or at the Hunterian Museum, University of Glasgow. This has often led to the recognition of details not hitherto visible. Traces of the original red paint have been observed in the letters of several inscriptions and on their sculptured panels (see nos. 68, 110, 137). The readings of the inscriptions follow *RIB*, except where further scrutiny, or cleaning, or both, have suggested alternatives.[1]

Dating criteria

The total period of Roman occupation of Scotland (Birrens and Newstead being the exceptions—see below) lasted for hardly more than 40-50 years. The occupation falls into three distinct phases; hence there is a particular value for students of Roman Britain. In the later first century AD (or Flavian period) the forts were built principally of timber, and the records erected to commemorate their construction would probably have been of wood. Only a single gravestone (undecorated, and so omitted here) can, with plausibility, be assigned to the Flavian period in Scotland.[2] It may be, however, that some altars, religious sculpture, or gravestones, from forts occupied in both Flavian and Antonine periods belong to the former; it has therefore been considered safer in the following pages to designate all such material as '1st/2nd century AD'. It has been assumed that material deriving from forts which (as far as we are aware) were occupied only in the Antonine period, should be assigned to that period, even if there is no dating evidence. Certainly, many stones, from their reference to the emperor Antoninus, their use of particular formulae or name-forms, or from their lettering, can be seen to belong to the second century. Others, however, provide no such guidance. The attempted occupation in the Severan period was so brief, and so restricted geographically, that only a small number of stones can be attributed to it.

A concentration of material will be noted at the fort-site of Birrens in south-west Scotland. Birrens has yielded almost one-quarter of all the items considered in the following pages. The main reason for this is the length of occupation of the fort. A turf-and-timber Flavian fort was succeeded by a stone-built Hadrianic fort, which served as an outpost for Hadrian's Wall. This was then rebuilt at the beginning of the Antonine period, and reconstructed on one further occasion in AD 158. It remained in use until at least AD 180. The fort-site, relatively undisturbed over the centuries on rough ground, was subjected to comprehensive excavation in 1895; further work (which yielded little for our purpose) took place in 1936-7 and 1962-9.[3] All the internal buildings were of stone. Most of the dated sculptural material belongs to the final period of occupation, from AD 158 onwards, when the Second Cohort of *Tungri* formed the garrison, and had at its disposal, or within its ranks, craftsmen of unusual ability and imagination. Other material, almost certainly deriving from the earlier phases, was in part re-used as building stone in the final period. By contrast, Newstead on the Tweed, the largest fort

[1] L. J. F. Keppie, 'Roman Inscriptions from Scotland: some Additions and Corrections to *RIB*', *PSAS* cxiii, 1983, forthcoming.

[2] *RIB* 2213.

[3] D. Christison *et al.*, *PSAS* xxx, 1895-6, pp. 81-199; E. B. Birley, *PSAS* lxxii, 1937-8, pp. 275-347; A. S. Robertson, *Birrens (Blatobulgium)* Edinburgh, 1975.

in Scotland (apart from the legionary bases at Inchtuthil and Carpow), which like Birrens was mostly stone-built, and remained in use into the later second century AD, has yielded disappointingly little in the way of sculptured stonework. However, a wealth of spectacular small finds, including parade-armour (see nos. 54–6) and military equipment, was recovered during excavation in 1905–9.[1]

The identity of the sculptors

Throughout the Roman period, Scotland remained a military zone, seemingly under the army's direct rule. The surviving structural remains are the army's forts, camps, and defensive works in a hostile countryside. The majority of stones, it is clear, were erected or commissioned by the army, to commemorate the achievements of individual units, to testify to the religious beliefs and practices of the soldiers and their families, or to commemorate dead comrades. Outside the forts, there grew up small settlements populated by civilians, but the epigraphic record of such communities remains slight.[2] It can hardly be doubted that the majority of surviving stones was produced by masons either serving in, or commissioned by, the army.

The legions were present in force at the conquest stage of each occupation, but the garrison-units were mostly regiments of auxiliaries. In the Flavian period a legion, apparently the Twentieth, was established at Inchtuthil, and in the Severan phase, men from the Second or the Sixth legions (or both), were based at Carpow. There is a growing body of evidence which suggests that small groups of legionaries served as garrisons in a number of Antonine Wall forts,[3] but for the most part the legions returned to their bases in the south once the conquest was complete. Before leaving, however, they made a substantial contribution towards the construction of the frontier works and the garrison posts which the auxiliaries were to occupy. Sometimes an inscription provides the record, sometimes an emblem—the capricorn or pegasus of the Second Legion, and the Boar of the Twentieth (see nos. 41, 49–51, 58, 123, 137, 146, 148–9, 152, 154, 156–7). The Sixth Legion, however, made little use of emblems (see no. 25).

The commemorative records left by the legions provide a sizeable proportion of the sculptured material from Scotland. Some incorporate scenes illustrating battles fought, or warrior tribesmen vanquished. The survival from the line of the Antonine Wall of so many of the distance slabs (perhaps one-third or more of all those erected)[4] is particularly valuable; many are equal in execution to much that has survived from areas far to the South. The apparent care and attention exercised by their sculptors may testify to special pride in the extension of the province. Each of the legions had a distinctive style, and the products of its craftsmen are often instantly recognizable. The same designs recur, not always in expert hands. One sculptor working for the

[1] J. Curle, *A Roman Frontier Post and its People: the Fort of Newstead in the Parish of Melrose* Glasgow, 1911.

[2] P. Salway, *The Frontier People of Roman Britain* Cam-

bridge, 1965, pp. 155–64.

[3] L. J. F. Keppie, *Britannia* xiii, 1982, pp. 107 ff.

[4] Id., op. cit. (p. xiii, n. 6), p. 8.

Twentieth Legion produced six or more surviving stones from the four-mile stretch of the Antonine Wall between Castlehill and Old Kilpatrick.[1] Particular use was made by all the legions of the *pelta*-motif to flank an inscribed panel and emphasize its central importance.[2]

The styles of carving are typical of the Romano-Celtic amalgam so common in Britain, in both military and civilian contexts. There are sculptures of special distinction, and even beauty, but others are crude and rough in the extreme. Life-size sculpture in the round has not survived in quantity. Apart from a marble head (no. 57) and the leg of a bronze equestrian statue (no. 45) (both most probably loot from the South), such pieces as are known are religious in character, intended to ornament shrines, or to enhance the bathhouse buildings, upon which particular care was lavished.

The growth of Scottish museum collections

The earliest record of Roman stones in Scotland belongs to the mid sixteenth century, by which time many had already found their way to the country seats of landowners and noblemen, to be displayed to visitors as evidence of antiquarian enthusiasms. In 1695 the then Principal of Glasgow University persuaded many of these owners (some had been his students at Glasgow) to donate them to the University. These gifts formed the nucleus of the University's present collection, now housed in its Hunterian Museum. In 1768 the University published the *Monumenta Romani Imperii*, a series of etchings of its holdings.[3] The University's collection continued to expand throughout the nineteenth century and a detailed catalogue by James Macdonald appeared in 1897 under the title *Tituli Hunteriani*.

The extensive holdings of the National Museum of Antiquities of Scotland in Edinburgh had their origin in random gifts to the Society of Antiquaries from the 1780s onwards.[4] The growing fame of the collections, which then included many Egyptian, Etruscan, and Greek antiquities, and Roman inscriptions and sculpture from England, encouraged Sir George Clerk to donate in 1857 the many stones accumulated at Penicuik House by his ancestor Sir John Clerk.[5] Excavations conducted under the auspices of the Society of Antiquaries of Scotland from 1895 onwards at many major sites added to the collection.

In the present century the Hunterian Museum and the National Museum collections have continued to expand by the acquisition or donation of material found respectively in the West and East of Scotland, often from archaeological excavations,

---

[1] L. J. F. Keppie, *Scottish Archaeological Forum* vii, 1976, pp. 57–65.

[2] F. H. Thompson, *Ant. J.* xlviii, 1968, pp. 57–8.

[3] The date of initial publication, sometimes stated to have been 1771, is supplied (or at least narrowed) by the survival of a bill dated April 1768 presented to the University by the Foulis

Press for the engraving of the copperplates (now in Glasgow University Archives). A short supplement was added to the volume in 1771–2.

[4] A. S. Bell (ed.), *The Scottish Antiquarian Tradition* Edinburgh, 1981.

[5] *PSAS* iii, 1857–60, pp. 37–43.

carried out either by their own staffs, or under the auspices of the Ministry of Public Buildings and Works (later the Department of the Environment, and today the Scottish Development Department). Outside the main collections there is a small but impressive array of stones at Dumfries. Other pieces have been retained in local museums at Dundee, Perth, Melrose, and Falkirk. A few (see nos. 72, 82, 128) remain in private hands.

PART I

SCOTLAND SOUTH OF THE ANTONINE WALL

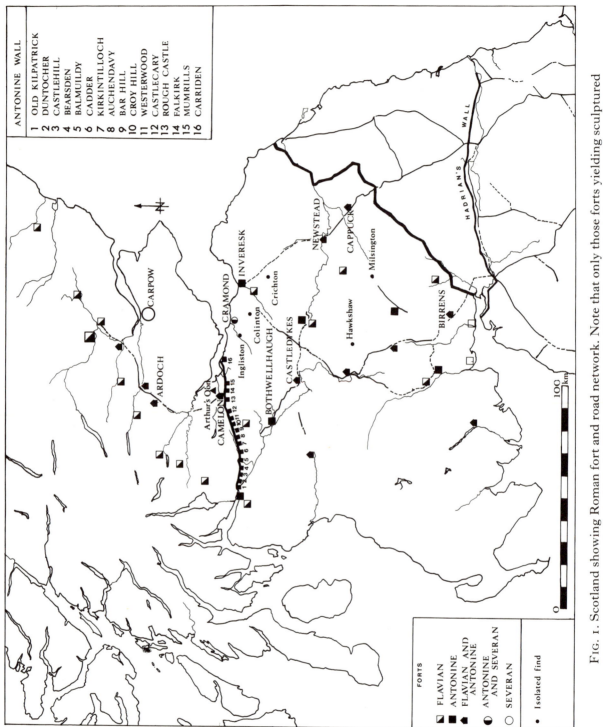

ANTONINE WALL

1 OLD KILPATRICK
2 DUNTOCHER
3 CASTLEHILL
4 BEARSDEN
5 BALMUILDY
6 CADDER
7 KIRKINTILLOCH
8 AUCHENDAVY
9 BAR HILL
10 CROY HILL
11 WESTERWOOD
12 CASTLECARY
13 ROUGH CASTLE
14 FALKIRK
15 MUMRILLS
16 CARRIDEN

FORTS

FLAVIAN
ANTONINE
FLAVIAN AND ANTONINE
ANTONINE AND SEVERAN
SEVERAN
• Isolated find

FIG. 1. Scotland showing Roman fort and road network. Note that only those forts yielding sculptured material considered in this volume are individually named on the map.

SCOTLAND SOUTH OF THE ANTONINE WALL

1 Altar to Di Deaeque Omnes   PLATE 1

Prov.: Birrens (*Blatobulgium*), Dumfriesshire, *c*.1812.

Loc.: National Museum of Antiquities of Scotland, Edinburgh. Inv. no. FV 3.

Wilson 1851, p. 398; Stuart 1852, p. 128 n.; *CIL* vii, 1074; Macdonald 1896, p. 158, no. 20 with fig. 27; Macdonald and Barbour 1897, p. 63, no. 16; *RIB* 2109; Robertson 1975, p. 98, no. 17.

The edges of the bolsters, *focus*, and shaft are worn and chipped.

H.: 0.7 m.; W.: 0.37 m.; D.: 0.11 m.

Letter heights: 1–3: 0.075 m.; 4: 0.07 m.; 5: 0.04 m.; 6: 0.025 m.

Relief carving. Local red sandstone.

The bolsters terminate in plain roundels with a central boss, and the *focus*-mount is squared off frontally. The *focus* itself is not hollowed out. *Focus*-mount and bolsters are set directly on top of the shaft. The die is bordered by a narrow moulding, decorated above and to the left and right with cable-patterns, but plain below. Incised below the final line of the inscription are two supine crescents symbolizing good fortune. The inscription reads: *Dib(us) De/ ab(us)q(ue) | omnib(us) | Frument/ius mil(es) coh(ortis) II/Tungr(orum)*.

The altar was erected by Frumentius, a soldier in the Second Cohort of *Tungri*, the garrison at Birrens in the Antonine II period.

Antonine date (after AD 158).

2 Altar to Disciplina   PLATE 1

Prov.: Birrens (*Blatobulgium*), Dumfriesshire, in the well of the headquarters building, during excavation of the fort-site, 1895.

Loc.: National Museum of Antiquities of Scotland, Edinburgh. Inv. no. FP 2.

Macdonald 1896, p. 130, no. 4 with fig. 9; B. Brown, *PSAS* xxx, 1895–6, pp. 172–7 with fig. 31; Macdonald and Barbour 1897, p. 66 with pls. i.2 and ii.1 and 2; R. Munro, *PSA* ser. 2, xvi, 1896, p. 195; *EE* ix, 1228; T. Ross, in Macdonald and Park 1906, pp. 142–4; RCAHMS 1920, p. 164 with fig. 113; *RIB* 2092; Robertson 1975, p. 97, no. 11.

The *focus* and corners of the capital, shaft, and base have suffered damage. Parts of the bolsters, probably broken away at the moment of discovery, have been roughly repaired.

H.: 0.98 m.; W.: 0.57 m.; D.: 0.46 m.

Letter heights: 1–4: 0.09 m.; 5: 0.08 m.

Relief carving. Local red sandstone.

Centrally placed on the front of the capital is a door topped by an arch which springs from plain chamfered imposts set upon single columns. The column-shafts are composed of flanged reels which sit upon plain chamfered bases. The impost capitals support a triple-ribbed cornice, the outermost moulding of which is decorated with cable-patterns. Between the columns are two panelled doors topped by horizontal bands of chevrons and cable-patterns which form the lintel. In the dome of the arch, shell-like striations radiate from the keystone. Three horizontal bands of chevron and reel motifs, which extend continuously around the lower part of the capital, may have been intended to suggest a dado.[1] The bolsters on the front of the capital terminate in eight-petalled rosettes. A line of cable-patterns links the bolsters and *focus*-mount. On the left and right faces of the capital three additional bolster-terminals protrude from the main cylinders, each terminating in an eight-petalled rosette. On the rear face, centrally placed between two small four-petalled rosettes, is a small vessel, of which the upper part is broken away. The *focus* simulates a metal dish with central boss and twisted wire handles, one of which is lost.

---

[1] Cf. *RIB* 1210, 1212; Phillips 1977, nos. 185, 186.

Capital and shaft are demarcated by a line of modil-lions, and the shaft and base by a line of cable-patterns; both mouldings extend round the four faces of the altar. On the left face of the shaft is a *patera* with a prominent central boss decorated with an incised cross and an ornamented handle terminating in a ram's head. On the right face are a cleaver and an axe. The inscription reads: *Discip(linae)* / *Aug(usti)* / *coh(ors) II* / *Tungr(orum)* / *mil(liaria) eq(uitata)* *c(ivium) L(atinorum).*[1]

The findspot of this altar, which is one of the most highly decorated and accomplished known in Britain, suggests that it once stood in the chapel of the headquarters building.[2] It was erected by the cohort known to have formed the garrison at Birrens in the Antonine II period.

Antonine date (after AD 158).

3   Altar to Fortuna   PLATE 2

Prov.: Birrens (*Blatobulgium*), Dumfriesshire, before 1772.

Loc.: National Museum of Antiquities of Scotland, Edinburgh. Inv. no. FV 4.

Pennant 1776, ii, p. 408, no. 3; Wilson 1851, p. 399; Gough 1806, iv, p. 62; Hodgson 1840, p. 253, no. ccxlvii.7; Stuart 1852, p. 128; C. Roach Smith, *Collectanea Antiqua* iii, 1854, p. 204, pl. xxxiii.3; *CIL* vii, 1063; *EE* ix, p. 613; Macdonald 1896, p. 147, no. 14 with fig. 19; Macdonald and Barbour 1897, pp. 58-9, no. 10; RCAHMS 1920, p. 165 with fig. 115; *RIB* 2093; Robertson 1975, p. 97, no. 8.

The mouldings on the capital and base are chipped and worn.

H.: 1.19 m.; W.: 0.47 m.; D.: 0.31 m.

Letter heights: 1-5: 0.075 m.

Relief carving. Local red sandstone.

A plain incised line connects the bolsters on the front of the capital by way of three undulating mouldings. The inscription reads: *Fortunae* / *coh(ors) I* / *Nervana* / *Germanor(um)* / *(milliaria) eq(uitata).*

It seems likely that the First Nervian Cohort of *Germani* formed the garrison at Birrens in the Antonine I period.[3]

Antonine date (AD 142–*c*.157).

4   Base and Statue of Fortuna   PLATE 2

Prov.: Birrens (*Blatobulgium*), Dumfriesshire, *c*.1772.

Now lost (illustration from Pennant).

Pennant 1776, p. 407, App. viii, pl. xlv; Gough 1806, iv, p. 62, pl. i.7; Hodgson 1840, p. 253, no. ccxlviii.8; Wilson 1851, p. 397; Stuart 1852, p. 129, pl. ii.6; McCaul 1863, p. 246; *CIL* vii, 1064; *EE* ix, p. 614; Macdonald 1896, pp. 144-5, no. 12, fig. 17; RCAHMS 1920, p. 102 with pl. (fig. 76); *RIB* 2094; Robertson 1975, p. 97, no. 11.

As drawn by Pennant, the statue survived up to waist height, but R. G. Collingwood's drawing (1928) shows only the ankles and feet above the base.

No measurements given.

Statue carved in the round. Type of stone not recorded.

Set on an inscribed base was a female statue wearing a long tunic with an overfold flaring at the knee. The inscription read: *Fortunae [pro]* / *salute P(ubli)* *Campa[ni]* / *Italici praef(ecti) coh I[I]* / *Tun(grorum)* *Celer libertus* / *v(otum) s(olvit) l(aetus) l(ibens)* *m(erito).*

The statue (presumably of the goddess Fortuna) and the base were erected by a freedman of P. Campanius Italicus, prefect of the Second Cohort of *Tungri*, the garrison at Birrens in the Antonine II period.

Antonine date (after AD 158).

5   Altar to Jupiter   PLATE 2

Prov.: Sprinkell, 3 km east of Birrens, Dumfriesshire, 1814.

Now lost (illustration from *Scots Magazine*).

Scots Magazine lxxix, 1817, p. 367 with fig., quoting from W. S. Irvine, *The History of the Antiquities of Dumfriesshire c.*1815 (MS formerly in Library of Society of Antiquaries of Scotland; not now trace-able); Wilson 1851, p. 400; *CIL* vii, 1067; *EE* ix, p. 614; Macdonald 1896, p. 160 n. 2, no. 1; *RIB* 2098; Robertson 1975, p. 98, no. 22.

The top left-hand corner of the shaft had evidently suffered some damage. No base is shown.

H.: 0.71 m.; W.: 0.405 m.; D.: —.

---

[1] This expansion of the letters C L follows *RIB*; for an alternative, see H. Wolf, *Chiron* vi, 1976, pp. 267-80.

[2] For the military cult of *Discip(u)lina*, see I. A. Richmond, *AA* ser. 4, xxi, 1943, pp. 165-9; P. S. Austen and D. J. Breeze, *AA* ser. 5, vii, 1979, pp. 115-26.

[3] See Robertson 1975, p. 95, no. 1 for a fragment of an inscription mentioning the cohort, found during the 1962-9 excavations, stratified below an Antonine II road.

Relief carving. Type of stone not recorded.

The *focus* took the form of a plain two-handled dish. At the top four corners of the capital were quarter-circles, apparently incised. On the right face of the shaft was a *patera*, with its handle pointing downwards. It may be assumed that the decorative features had been somewhat simplified in the copying. The inscription read: [I(ovi)] O(ptimo) M(aximo) / ....]inius / .....] fecit pr[.......

The altar was erected to Jupiter, but the name of the dedicator cannot be restored. The letters PR might indicate that he was commander (*praefectus*) of the cohort in garrison at the fort.

1st/2nd century AD.

6 Altar to Mars or the Matres   PLATE 2

Prov.: Birrens (*Blatobulgium*), Dumfriesshire, before 1886.

Now lost (illustration from Macdonald).

W. T. Watkin, *Arch. J.* xliv, 1887, p. 122; *EE* vii, 1091; Macdonald 1896, p. 155, no. 17 with fig. 24; Macdonald and Barbour 1897, p. 62; *RIB* 2101; Robertson 1975, p. 98, no. 24.

Only the top left-hand corner of the altar was recorded, showing one bolster and a small part of the die.

H.: 0.405 m.; W.: 0.265 m.; D.: 0.085 m.

Relief carving. Type of stone not recorded.

The surviving bolster terminated in a six-pointed rosette. An incised semi-circle filled the gap between the bolster and the *focus*-mount which was occupied by a similar rosette. Some attempt had been made to suggest cornice mouldings on the left side of the shaft. Given the lack of depth to the stone there is unlikely to have been a *focus*. The inscription read: *Ma*[........] / *Sa*[......... / ....

Whether the altar was dedicated to Mars or to the Matres (Mother Goddesses) cannot be determined. Similarities in style suggest that it was the work of craftsmen of the Second Cohort of *Tungri*, the garrison at Birrens in the Antonine II period.

Antonine period (perhaps after AD 158)?

7 Altar to Mars and Victory   PLATE 3

Prov.: Birrens (*Blatobulgium*), Dumfriesshire, c.1812.

Loc.: National Museum of Antiquities of Scotland, Edinburgh. Inv. no. FV 2.

Wilson 1851, p. 398 with fig.; Stuart 1852, p. 128; C. Roach Smith, *Collectanea Antiqua* iii, 1854, p. 202, pl. xxxiii; McCaul 1863, p. 244; *CIL* vii, 1068; *ILS* 2555; Macdonald 1896, pp. 155-7, no. 18 with fig. 25; Macdonald and Barbour 1897, p. 62, no. 14; RCAHMS 1920, p. 164 with fig. 114; *RIB* 2100; Robertson 1975, p. 97, no. 13; Clarke, Breeze, and Mackay 1980, p. 74, no. 81.

The altar has sustained slight damage to the mouldings on its capital and base and at the corners of the shaft. The front face of the shaft is scored and scuffed.

H.: 1.365 m.; W.: 0.59 m.; D.: 0.34 m.

Letter heights: 1-3: 0.055 m.; 4: 0.05 m.; 5: 0.055 m.

Relief carving. Local red sandstone. The back of the altar has been left rough.

The front faces of the capital and of the base have been extensively carved by a competent craftsman. The bolsters terminate in six-pointed rosettes, between which are three semi-circles in relief; above the central semi-circle are two supine crescents. On the front of the capital, within a plain narrow moulding, is a frieze of five ivy leaves, their tips pointing to the left. The front of the base is similarly ornamented with ivy leaves, eight in all, arranged in pairs, with the tips pointing away to left and right. The inscription reads: *Marti et Victo/riae Aug(usti) c(ives) Rae/ti milit(antes) in coh(orte) / II Tungr(orum) cui / praeest Silvius / Auspex praef(ectus) / v(otum) s(olverunt) l(ibentes) / m(erito)*. Ivy leaves, matching those on the capital and base, and a centrally placed motif of four concentric circles, serve as word-stops in the final line.

The inscription provides evidence for the presence in the Second Cohort of *Tungri* of Raetian tribesmen, presumably recruited to a detachment serving in Raetia earlier in the Antonine period.[1]

Antonine date (after AD 158).

8 Statue-base to Mercury   PLATE 3

Prov.: Birrens (*Blatobulgium*), Dumfriesshire, in the ruins of a small building west of the fort-site, 1731, together with no. 12 and *RIB* 2103.

Loc.: National Museum of Antiquities of Scotland, Edinburgh. Inv. no. FV 6.

Sir John Clerk, letter to R. Gale, October 1731,

---

[1] E. B. Birley, *CW*, N.S. xxxv, 1935, pp. 56-60; R. W. Davies, *Epigr. Stud.* 4, 1967, pp. 108-11.

Surtees Soc. lxxx (= Stukeley, *Memoirs and Corre-spondence* iii), 1887, pp. 398-9; Gordon 1732, p. 28, pl. lxviii.2; Horsley 1732, pp. 342, 354, pl. (*Scotland*) xxxv; J. Clerk, *Dissertatio de monumentis quibusdam Romanis* 1750, fig. 2; Hodgson 1840, p. 252, no. ccxliii.2; Gough 1806, iv, p. 61, pl. i, fig. 2; Pennant 1776, ii, p. 409; Stuart 1852, p. 126, pl. ii.4; *CIL* vii, 1069 with *Addit.* p. 313; *ILS* 7316a; Macdonald 1896, pp. 136-8, no. 7; Macdonald and Barbour 1897, p. 53, no. 3; *RIB* 2102; Robertson 1975, p. 98, no. 5.

H.: 0.78 m.; W.: 0.47 m.; D.: 0.29 m.

Letter heights: 1-5: 0.05 m.; 6: 0.03 m.

Relief carving. Local buff sandstone.

The corners of the capital and the shaft are chipped and worn. The right side of the shaft is much more weathered than the left side, but whether this is the result of exposure to the elements in ancient or more modern times is not known.

Decoration is confined to the left and right sides of the shaft. On the left is a cock perched on a small globe above an elaborate rosette in high relief. On the right side are two sacrificial implements: a jug and a *patera* with a central boss and a handle terminating in an animal-head. The inscription reads: *Deo Mercu/rio Iul(ius) Cres/cens sigill(um) | collign(io) cult(orum) | eius d(e) s(uo) d(edit) | v(otum) s(olvit) l(ibens) m(erito)*.

The base records the donation of a cult-statue to Mercury, which was presumably placed in the rectangular hollow in the top. The cock and the rosette both have chthonic significance, and point to Mercury's role as guide of the souls to the underworld.

1st/2nd century AD (probably Hadrianic-Antonine date).

9   Altar to Minerva   PLATE 4

Prov.: Birrens (*Blatobulgium*), Dumfriesshire, in the field west of the fort-site, 1810.

Loc.: Dumfries Museum. Inv. no. 1950/53/1.

Dumfries and Galloway Courier 31 Aug. 1813 with fig.: ibid. 7 Sept. 1813; Wilson 1851, p. 397, quoting W. S. Irvine, *The History of the Antiquities of Dumfriesshire c.*1815 (MS in the Library of the Society of Antiquaries of Scotland, Edinburgh; not now traceable); A. J. K., *Gent. Mag.* cii, 1832, i, p. 603; Stuart 1852, p. 128, n. (*b*), no. 4; McCaul 1863, p. 245; *CIL* vii, 1071; T. Hodgkin, *AA* ser. 2, xii, 1887, pp. 102-11; *EE* vii, 1090; Macdonald 1896, pp. 153-4, no. 16 with figs. 21-3; Macdonald and Barbour 1897, pp. 60-1, fig. 4; A. E. Truckell, *TDGNHAS* ser. 3, xxix, 1950-1, p. 139; *RIB* 2104; Robertson 1975, p. 97, no. 14.

Slight damage has been sustained to the corners of the capital, shaft, and base.

H.: 1.244 m.; W.: 0.43 m.; D.: 0.305 m.

Letter heights: 1: 0.065 m.; 2-4: 0.05 m.; 5: 0.045 m.; 6: 0.035 m.; 7: 0.045 m.

Relief carving. Local yellow-grey sandstone.

The bolsters terminate in six-pointed rosettes; the *focus*-mount is occupied by a supine crescent, supported on a low pedestal. On the front of the capital, within a narrow plain moulding, are two leaping dolphins, whose snouts meet over a disc formed by three concentric circles. The top left and top right corners of the panel are occupied by ravens facing outwards. On the left and right faces of the capital, shaft, and base are designs of twisting ivy tendrils set within plain narrow mouldings. On the front of the base two dolphins leap upwards and apart; between them is a raven facing left. The inscription reads: *Deae | Minervae | coh(ors) II Tun/grorum | mil(liaria) eq(uitata) c(ivium) L(atinorum)*[1] *| cui praeest C(aius) Silv(ius) | Auspex praef(ectus)*.

It is possible that the dolphins symbolize the provincial Minerva's association with water, while the ravens indicate her role as goddess of war.[2] The Second Cohort of *Tungri* formed the garrison at Birrens in the Antonine II period.

Antonine date (after AD 158).

10   Head of Minerva? within Niche   PLATE 4

Prov.: Birrens (*Blatobulgium*), Dumfriesshire, during excavation of the fort-site, 1895.

Loc.: National Museum of Antiquities of Scotland, Edinburgh. Inv. no. FP 8.

Macdonald 1896, p. 197; Macdonald and Barbour 1897, pl. iiiA, fig. 22; Robertson 1975, p. 99, no. 36.

The nose, chin, and forehead are damaged, and the edges of the fragment are chipped and worn.

H.: 0.1 m.; W.: 0.19 m.; D.: 0.045 m.

Relief carving. Local red sandstone.

---

[1] Cf. above, no. 2.   [2] Cf. Ross 1967, pp. 190, 244-9.

Within a gabled niche is a human head, apparently female, tilted upwards and to the right, with full lips, protruding eyes, and wavy hair. She wears a helmet, with a crest falling away to the left. To the right, at an awkward angle, is the top of what may be the shaft of a spear or torch.

The figure may represent Minerva, goddess of war, standing within a niche (cf. no. 12 below).

1st/2nd century AD (probably Hadrianic-Antonine date).

11 Relief of ?Priapus   PLATE 4

Prov.: Probably Birrens (*Blatobulgium*), Dumfriesshire, before 1810.[1]

Loc.: National Museum of Antiquities of Scotland, Edinburgh. Inv. no. FV 19.

Arch. Scot. iii, 1831, App. p. 92; NMAS *Catalogue* 1849, p. 70, no. 4E; Stuart 1852, p. 135 n.; *CIL* vii, 1079; Macdonald 1896, pp. 149–52, no. 15 with fig. 20; Macdonald and Barbour 1897, pp. 59–60, no. 11; *RIB* 2106; W. Dodds, *TDGNHAS* xlix, 1972, pp. 35–9; Robertson 1975, p. 98, no. 28.

The corners of the slab are broken away; its surface is badly flaked and worn and much of the inscription lost.

H.: 0.25 m.; W.: 0.28 m.; D.: 0.06 m.

Letter heights: 1: *c*.0.025 m.

Relief carving. Local yellow-buff sandstone.

The stone bears the head of a man facing the front. Horns emerge from his forehead and curve backwards. The inscription reads: [*P*]*riapi m*(*entula?*).

The inscription has usually been thought to indicate a dedication to Priapus, the Roman god of fertility, but Anne Ross believes the head to be that of a Celtic deity, perhaps the Gaulish Erriapus.[2]

1st/2nd century AD.

12 Relief of Brigantia   PLATE 4

Prov.: Birrens (*Blatobulgium*), Dumfriesshire, in the ruins of a small building west of the fort-site (probably within the annexe), 1731, together with no. 8 and *RIB* 2103.

Loc.: National Museum of Antiquities of Scotland, Edinburgh. Inv. no. FV 5.

J. Clerk, letter to R. Gale, October 1731, *Surtees Soc.* lxxx (= Stukeley, *Memoirs and Correspondence* iii), 1887, pp. 395–8; Horsley 1732, pp. 341, 355, pl. (*Scotland*) xxxiv; Gordon 1732, p. 27, pl. lxviii.1; J. Clerk, *Dissertatio de monumentis quibusdam Romanis* 1750, pp. 7–8, fig. 1; Pennant 1776, ii, p. 409, no. 14; W. Camden, *Britannia*, ed. R. Gough, 1789, p. 323; Hodgson 1840, p. 252, no. ccxlii.1; Stuart 1852, p. 124, pl. ii.3; C. L. Grotefend, *BJ* xviii, 1852, pp. 238–9; McCaul 1863, p. 237; *CIL* vii, 1062; *ILS* 4718; Macdonald 1896, p. 133 with fig. 11; Macdonald and Barbour 1897, p. 52, no. 2; RCAHMS 1920, p. 165 with fig. 116; E. B. Birley, *PSAS* lxxii, 1937–8, p. 279; G. Macdonald, ibid. lxxiii, 1938–9, p. 261; N. Jolliffe, *Arch. J.* xcviii, 1941, pp. 36–61; *RIB* 2091; Toynbee 1962, p. 157, no. 80, pl. 77; 1964, pp. 174–5; Ross 1967, pp. 216–17; Robertson 1975, p. 98, no. 19; Clarke, Breeze, and Mackay 1980, p. 73, no. 80.

Slight damage has been sustained to the upper left and right corners of the niche, and to the spear-shaft just below its head.

H.: 0.91 m.; W.: 0.44 m.; D.: 0.22 m.

Letter heights: 1: 0.035 m.; 2: 0.02 m.

Relief carving. Local buff sandstone. At the time of discovery, gold leaf was said to be visible in places on the stone, but it has now disappeared.

Within a gabled niche a winged female figure stands facing the front. In her left hand she holds a globe at waist level, and in her right a spear which rests in the crook of her right arm. She wears a tunic which falls to her feet and is secured at the right shoulder by a circular brooch. Over her shoulders is a long cloak. On her breast is a gorgon-head medallion. She wears a triple-plumed helmet encircled by a mural crown; there are horn-like projections on either side of the helmet. To her left, part of an oval or circular shield protrudes from behind her cloak and rests against the niche; a horizontal hand-grip can be seen close to the right-hand margin of the shield. To her right, on the lower-left respond of the niche, is a conical omphalos-stone. The inscription reads: *Brigantiae s*(*acrum*) *Amandus* | *arc*(*h*)*itectus ex imperio imp*(*eratum*) [*f*(*ecit*)].[3]

---

[1] For a discussion of the provenance, see Macdonald 1896, p. 149.

[2] A. Ross, *AA* ser. 4, xxxix, 1961, p. 80.

[3] The precise reading of the second line of the inscription, and its meaning, have always been in doubt; see R. P. Wright, on *RIB* 2091.

The figure represents Brigantia, tutelary goddess of the Brigantes, whose tribal territory covered much of northern England. The spear, shield, and gorgon-medallion are appropriate to Minerva, goddess of war, while the wings imply a degree of identification with Victory, and the globe and omphalos-stone are attributes of Juno Caelestis. The turreted crown suggests a role as protectress of her tribe, or of a major city.

The dedication was made by Amandus, a military engineer (*architectus*), perhaps a member of the Birrens garrison, who has been tentatively identified with a Valerius Amandus, a legionary *architectus* attested in Lower Germany in AD 209.[1] The partial assimilation to Juno Caelestis has been held to show the influence of Julia Domna, wife of the emperor Septimius Severus,[2] and it seemed reasonable to date the stone to the Severan period. However, recent excavations at Birrens have revealed no material necessarily later than *c.* AD 180,[3] so that the dedication presumably belongs (at the latest) to the Antonine period.

Hadrianic-Antonine date?

13   Altar to Harimella   PLATE 5

Prov.: Birrens (*Blatobulgium*), Dumfriesshire, before 1772.

Loc.: Dumfries Museum. Inv. no. 1951/31/1.

Pennant 1776, ii, p. 406, pl. xlv; Gough 1806, iv, p. 62, pl. i.5; Hodgson 1840, p. 253, no. ccxlvi.5; K. F. Hermann, *Göttingische gelehrte Anzeigen* 1846, pp. 1413-21; Stuart 1852, p. 128, pl. ii.1; C. Roach Smith, *Collectanea Antiqua* iii, 1854, p. 203; McCaul 1863, p. 239; *CIL* vii, 1065; *EE* ix, p. 614; *ILS* 4744; Macdonald 1896, p. 141, no. 10 with fig. 15; Macdonald and Barbour 1897, p. 55, no. 6; RCAHMS 1920, p. 165 with fig. 117; A. E. Truckell, *TDGNHAS* ser. 3, xxix, 1950-1, p. 139; *RIB* 2096; Robertson 1975, p. 98, no. 21.

The corners of the bolsters are damaged and the altar is weathered; the inscription is now very faint.

H.: 0.685 m.; W.: 0.355 m.; D.: 0.305 m.

Letter heights: 1: 0.055 m.; 2-4: 0.045 m.; 5: 0.035 m.

Relief carving. Local yellowish-grey sandstone.

The bolsters terminate in six-pointed rosettes; between them, on the *focus*-mount, is a small four-petalled rosette. The sides of the shaft are plain. The inscription reads: *Deae | Harimel/lae sac(rum) Ga/midiahus | arc(h)it(ectus) v(otum) s(olvit) l(aetus) l(ibens) m(erito)*.

The goddess Harimella is not otherwise known, but is assumed to belong to the Rhineland, from which both garrison-cohorts at Birrens were originally drawn. Gamidiahus was presumably a member of one of these cohorts. Given the similarities in the style of carving to no. 7, this altar may have been the work of craftsmen of the Second Cohort of *Tungri*.

Antonine date (perhaps after AD 158?).

14   Dedication to Maponus?   PLATE 5

Prov.: Birrens (*Blatobulgium*), Dumfriesshire, during excavation of Building IX/X, unstratified, 1967.

Loc.: Hunterian Museum, University of Glasgow.

R. P. Wright, *JRS* lviii, 1968, p. 209, no. 28, pl. xix.2; Robertson 1975, p. 95, no. 3 with pl. 10 and fig. 25.3.

The slab is damaged at its edges, and parts of the surface of the stone, especially at the bottom-left corner, have broken away.

H.: 0.33 m.; W.: 0.55 m.; D.: 0.08 m.

Letter heights: 1: 0.01-0.02 m.

Incised with a pointed instrument. Local red sandstone.

This flat slab may once have formed part of the paved floor of Building IX/X. It bears on its upper surface the incised figure of an animal, facing right, ears erect, with a collar around its neck. The legs are each indicated by a single line. The body is marked by a series of angled lines. The inscription, in cursive script, and set at right angles to the animal-figure, has been read as *Cistumuci lo(co) Mabomi*.

The identification of the animal and the nature of the dedication remain in doubt. If the axis of the stone *is* horizontal, the animal can be seen as a dog resembling a terrier,[4] or, if vertical, as a serpent.[5] The inscription may refer to a Cistumucus, from *Locus*

---

[1] S. N. Miller, *JRS* xxvii, 1937, p. 208.
[2] Toynbee 1962, loc. cit.
[3] Robertson 1975, p. 286.
[4] For the species, perhaps distinctively British, see Toynbee 1962, p. 150, no. 59, pl. 62; ead., *Animals in Roman Life and Art* 1973, p. 104, pl. 42; p. 365 n. 32.
[5] For the significance of the serpent in Celtic tradition, see Ross 1967, pp. 344-8.

Maponi, a place-name inferred from an entry in the Ravenna Cosmography[1] and tentatively identified with Lochmaben, 15 km north-west of Birrens fort.[2] Alternatively, the slab may commemorate an offering or vow to the god Maponus, a Celtic deity sometimes equated with Apollo, and recorded several times in the northern frontier region.[3] In Welsh vernacular tradition dogs are associated with Maponus (or Mabon) in his capacity as a hunting god.[4] Animal and inscription may have been carved by a member of the Birrens garrison, but the circumstances cannot be imagined.

Antonine date?

15 Altar to Ricagambeda PLATE 5

Prov.: Birrens (*Blatobulgium*), Dumfriesshire, *c*.1812.

Loc.: National Museum of Antiquities, Edinburgh. Inv. no. FV1.

Wilson 1851, p. 399; C. Roach Smith, *Collectanea Antiqua* iii, 1854, p. 202, pl. xxxiii; Stuart 1852, p. 128 n.; McCaul 1863, pp. 240–1; *CIL* vii, 1072; *ILS* 4752; Macdonald 1896, p. 157, no. 19 with fig. 26; Macdonald and Barbour 1897, p. 62; *RIB* 2107; Robertson 1975, p. 98, no. 15.

A small segment has been cut away from the lower right-hand corner of the base. The bolsters and the corners of the capital and shaft are chipped.

H.: 1.12 m.; W.: 0.432 m.; D.: 0.28 m.

Letter heights: 1–5: 0.05 m.

Relief carving. Local red sandstone.

Decoration is confined to the capital; the bolsters terminate in seven-pointed rosettes. Incised lines emphasize the undulations of the *focus*-mount. The raised central boss of the *focus* is decorated with vertical ribbing, perhaps simulating a metal vessel or cap. On the sides of each bolster are two raised circular bosses. The inscription reads: *Deae Ricagam/bedae pagus | Vellaus milit(ans) | coh(orte) II Tung(rorum) | v(otum) s(olvit) l(ibens) m(erito)*.

The goddess Ricagambeda and the *pagus Vellaus*

are not otherwise recorded, but both may belong in the Rhineland,[5] home of the Second Cohort of *Tungri*, the garrison at Birrens in the Antonine II period.

Antonine date (after AD 158).

16 Altar to Viradecthis PLATE 6

Prov.: Birrens (*Blatobulgium*), Dumfriesshire, before 1772.

Loc.: Dumfries Museum. Inv. no. 1951/31/2.

Pennant 1776, ii, p. 406, pl. xlv; Gough 1806, iv, p. 324; Hodgson 1840, p. 253, no. ccxlvii.6; Stuart 1852, p. 128, pl. ii.2; C. Roach Smith, *Collectanea Antiqua* iii, 1854, pp. 202–3; McCaul 1863, p. 240; *CIL* vii, 1073; *EE* ix, p. 614; *ILS* 4756; Macdonald 1896, pp. 142–4, no. 11 with fig. 16; Macdonald and Barbour 1897, p. 6; A. E. Truckell, *TDGNHAS* ser. 3, xxix, 1950–1, p. 139; *RIB* 2108; Robertson 1975, p. 98, no. 16.

The altar is badly weathered; there is a vertical crack across the capital and the die. Parts of the mouldings on the left and rear faces of the base are broken away. The capital does not sit squarely on the shaft, but is tilted to the right. The inscription is now very faint.

H.: 0.735 m.; W.: 0.46 m.; D.: 0.36 m.

Letter heights: 1–6: 0.045 m.

Relief carving. Local red sandstone.

The bolsters terminate in simple four-pointed rosettes, now much worn; between them on the *focus*-mount is a supine crescent supported on a small pyramid. The side and rear faces of the capital and shaft are plain. The inscription reads: *Deae Viradec/thi pa[g]us Con/drustis milit(ans) | in coh(orte) II Tun/gror(um) sub Silvi/o Auspice praef(ecto)*.

The altar was erected to the goddess Viradecthis by men of the *pagus Condrustis* serving in the Second Cohort of *Tungri*, the garrison at Birrens in the Antonine II period. The *pagus* can be localized in the Tungrian homeland on the Lower Rhine, where the goddess Viradecthis is also recorded.[6]

Antonine date (AD 158 onwards).

---

[1] I. A. Richmond and O. G. S. Crawford, *Archaeologia* xciii, 1949, p. 39.

[2] A. L. F. Rivet and C. Smith, *The Place-Names of Roman Britain* 1979, pp. 395–6.

[3] I. A. Richmond, *AA* ser. 4, xxi, 1943, pp. 206–10; D. J. Breeze and B. Dobson, *Hadrian's Wall* 1975, pp. 264–5.

[4] See, for example, P. K. Ford (ed.), *The Mabinogi and other Medieval Welsh Tales* 1979, p. 141. Dr L. C. Watson has suggested

a further intriguing possibility that the slab was a makeshift gravestone of the dog itself, the pet of one of the Birrens garrison; cf. J. M. C. Toynbee, *Animals in Roman Life and Art* 1973, pp. 109–10.

[5] E. B. Birley, *CW* ser. 2, xxxv, 1935, p. 56; R. W. Davies, *Epigr. Stud.* 4, 1967, p. 108.

[6] Macdonald 1896, loc. cit.; R. P. Wright, on *RIB* 2108; *ILS* 4756–7.

17   Uninscribed Altar   PLATE 6

Prov.: Birrens (*Blatobulgium*), Dumfriesshire, lying on steps leading down to a subterranean strongroom in the headquarters building, during excavation of the fort-site, 1895.

Loc.: National Museum of Antiquities of Scotland, Edinburgh. Inv. no. FP 4.

Macdonald 1896, pp. 132–3, no. 5, fig. 10; Macdonald and Barbour 1897, p. 64, no. 24, pl. ii.3; Robertson 1975, pp. 98–9, no. 31.

Some damage has been sustained to the mouldings on the base, to the corners of the capital and shaft, and to the bolster terminals.

H.: 0.905 m.; W.: 0.505 m.; D.: 0.34 m.

Relief carving. Local red sandstone.

Decoration is confined to the capital. The bolsters, each of which terminates in a simple roundel with a central boss, are decorated with sets of ribbed thunderbolts pointing to front and rear and separated by cable-patterned straps. A two-handled jug occupies the *focus*-mount. The *focus* itself is bordered by a cable-pattern. Below the bolsters a single band of upright acanthus leaves extends around the front and the sides of the capital; the rear face is plain.

Antonine date?[1]

18   Head of a God   PLATE 7

Prov.: Birrens (*Blatobulgium*), Dumfriesshire, before 1849.

Loc.: National Museum of Antiquities of Scotland, Edinburgh. Inv. no. FV 20.

NMAS *Catalogue* 1849, no. 3E; Anderson 1896, p. 198, fig. 50; W. Dodds, *TDGNHAS* ser. 3, xlix, 1972, pp. 35–8; Robertson 1975, p. 99, no. 38.

The head is worn, and some damage has been sustained by the nose and right cheek.

H.: 0.175 m.; W.: 0.10 m.; D.: 0.105 m.

Carved in the round. Creamy-buff limestone.

The head is male. The eyes and eyelids are indicated by deeply incised lines. The mouth is small, with the corners upturned to produce a slightly amused expression. The hair is all but hidden by a tight-fitting animal-skin cap. An animal-head (perhaps that of a wild cat)[2] is visible above the forehead, together with traces of a slight crest, now mostly lost.

1st/2nd century AD (probably Hadrianic-Antonine date).

19   Head of a God

Prov.: Birrens (*Blatobulgium*), Dumfriesshire, *c*.1816. Now lost.

A. Hewison, letter to J. Barbour, reported in Macdonald and Barbour 1897, p. 15; J. M. C. Toynbee, *JRS* xlii, 1952, p. 63 n.

'A head of the Roman god Jupiter', presumably in stone, is reported to have been dug up at Birrens, during robbing of stone from the fort-site. Perhaps to be identified with no. 18 or no. 20, but there is no certainty.

1st/2nd century AD.

20   Head of a Goddess   PLATE 7

Prov.: Probably Birrens (*Blatobulgium*), Dumfriesshire. The head was kept for many years at Burnfoot House near Birrens, along with two altars found within the annexe to the west of the fort-site (no. 9 and *RIB* 2103).

Loc.: Dumfries Museum, to which it was transferred in 1950. Inv. no. 1950/53/3.

A. E. Truckell, *TDGNHAS* ser. 3, xxix, 1950–1, p. 139; J. M. C. Toynbee, *JRS* xlii, 1952, pp. 63–5, pl. ix.2–3; *TDGNHAS* ser. 3, xxx, 1951–2, pp. 156–8; 1962, p. 147, no. 45, pl. 48; 1964, p. 104; A. S. Robertson, *Britannia* i, 1970, p. 221; W. Dodds, *TDGNHAS* ser. 3, xlix, 1972, pp. 35–8.

Parts of the nose and chin are broken away, and the right ear and 'bonnet-flap' are lost.

H.: 0.215 m.; W.: 0.165 m.; D.: 0.165 m.

Relief carving. Local whitish-grey sandstone.

The head is that of a female with smooth well-rounded features. The eyeballs are flattened and the mouth slightly down-turned. The hair is entirely concealed beneath a close-fitting cap or bonnet, whose flaps cover the ears.

Presumably the head belonged to a bust or statue,

---

[1] Similarities in style suggest that this altar was the work of craftsmen of the Second Cohort of *Tungri*, the garrison of the fort in the Antonine II period.

[2] Information from Miss Elspeth Scott and Dr D. Houston. A lion-head has been seen here by other commentators, which would suggest that the god be identified with Hercules.

of about two-thirds life-size, of a local goddess, which may have stood in the annexe or in the *vicus* outside the fort. J. M. C. Toynbee compares two heads from the Rhineland home of the Second Cohort of *Tungri*, which have head-dresses of similar type.

1st/2nd century AD (probably Hadrianic-Antonine date).

21　Head of a Deity　　PLATE 7

Prov.: Birrens (*Blatobulgium*), Dumfriesshire, in the annexe west of the fort-site, before 1857, probably *c*.1730.

Loc.: National Museum of Antiquities of Scotland, Edinburgh. Inv. no. FV 8.

PSAS iii, 1857–60, p. 42 no. (x); NMAS *Catalogue* 1869, p. 82, no. H153; Anderson 1896, p. 198 with fig. 49; W. Dodds, *TDGNHAS* ser. 3, xlix, 1972, pp. 35–9; Robertson 1975, p. 99, no. 37.

The head is somewhat worn, and the lower half of the face is blackened, perhaps by burning.

H.: 0.18 m.; W.: 0.14 m.; D.: 0.145 m.

Carved in the round. Local buff sandstone.

The eyes are lentoid and have strong brow-ridges. The hair, thick and roughly waved, hides the ears. The nose is wedge-shaped, and the mouth narrow, its corners downturned. The back of the head is noticeably flattened.

Presumably the head belonged to a bust or statue of about half life-size, probably of a local deity, but whether male or female is not clear.[1]

1st/2nd century AD (probably Hadrianic-Antonine date).

22　Tombstone of Soldier?　　PLATE 8

Prov.: Birrens (*Blatobulgium*), Dumfriesshire, in the ruins of a small building west of the fort-site; dug out on the orders of Sir John Clerk, 1733.

Now lost (illustration from Clerk).

Sir J. Clerk, letter to R. Gale, 1733, in *Surtees Soc.* lxxx (= Stukeley, *Memoirs and Correspondence* iii), 1887, p. 410; J. Clerk, *Dissertatio de monumentis quibusdam Romanis* 1750, pp. 15–16, with fig. 7; Gough 1806, iv, p. 61, pl. i.4; Hodgson 1840, p. 253;

Wilson 1851, p. 397; Stuart 1852, p. 127; Macdonald 1896, p. 139.

The head, hands, and feet of the figure, shown as carved separately and attached by dowels, were already lost when it was drawn. The slab was badly cracked.

No measurements are given, but in Clerk's drawing the slab fitted exactly on to the base *RIB* 2103, a dedication to Mercury.

Relief carving. Type of stone not recorded.

Within an arched niche was a full-length male figure, wearing a short-sleeved, belted tunic reaching to the knees.

The relief is likely to have been a gravestone, perhaps of a member of the Birrens garrison. Clerk, however, surmising from *RIB* 2103 that a statue of Mercury might originally have stood on the base, gave orders for a search to be made, and when this slab was brought to light, he at once claimed it as the missing 'statue'.

1st/2nd century AD (probably Hadrianic-Antonine date?).

23　Tombstone?　　PLATE 8

Prov.: Reported at Hoddom Castle, near the fort-site of Birrens (*Blatobulgium*), Dumfriesshire, 1772.

Now lost (illustration from Pennant).

Pennant 1776, ii, p. 407, pl. xlv; Macdonald 1896, p. 151 n.

Within a gabled niche is a human head, perhaps helmeted, with its neck set directly on the lower moulding.

Pennant's drawing shows what may have been the upper part of a tombstone commemorating a member of the Birrens garrison, unless the subject matter is religious; compare no. 10 above, with which Pennant's drawing has interesting similarities. There can, however, be no certainty over provenance, as at least one stone reported by Pennant at Hoddom Castle derived from a site on Hadrian's Wall (see below, p. 65).

1st/2nd century AD (probably Hadrianic-Antonine date?).

---

[1] Seen as female by the NMAS *Catalogue* and by subsequent commentators.

24   Pine-cone Finials

Prov.: On or near the fort-site at Birrens (*Blatobulgium*), Dumfriesshire, 1864; taken to the nearby farmhouse of Land.

Now lost.

W. Stevenson, *PSAS* xiii, 1878–9, pp. 268–9.

No measurements given.

Carved in the round. Type of stone not recorded.

Five pine-cone finials, each with a small pedestal below, were reported in the manuscript journal (now seemingly lost) of Sir Arthur Mitchell. Two apparently had their sides sliced down vertically.

1st/2nd century AD?

25   Building Record?   PLATE 8

Prov.: Birrens (*Blatobulgium*), Dumfriesshire, during excavation of the fort-site, 1895.

Loc.: National Museum of Antiquities of Scotland, Edinburgh. Inv. no. FP 5.

Macdonald 1896, p. 127, no. 1, fig. 6; Macdonald and Barbour 1897, p. 64, no. 20; *EE* ix, 1231; R. Munro, *PSA* xvi, 1895–7, p. 195, no. 1; *RIB* 2112; Robertson 1975, p. 95, no. 5.

The right-hand edge of the stone is broken away.

H.: 0.28 m.; W.: 0.28 m.; D.: 0.1 m.

Letter heights: 1: 0.045–0.05 m.

Relief carving. Local red sandstone.

This squarish slab, which seems too large and too thin (unless some part has flaked away) to be a building stone, bears the crudely incised inscription: *leg(io) VI Vi[c(trix)]*. To the left, below the inscription, are traces of what may be the head and body of a bovine animal, facing right. However, the traces could be the result of incomplete or casual dressing of the stone, and no sculptured motif may have been intended.

Hadrianic-Antonine date.

26   Fragments of Commemorative Slab, showing Victory-Figures   PLATE 9

Prov.: Birrens (*Blatobulgium*), Dumfriesshire. Fragment *a* was first reported in 1760, built into a wall at Hoddom Castle, Dumfriesshire, 6 km south-west of Birrens fort. Fragments *b* and *c* were recovered from the courtyard of the headquarters building, during excavation of the fort-site, 1895; fragment *d* was found during the same excavation, but no precise findspot is reported.

Loc.: National Museum of Antiquities of Scotland, Edinburgh. Inv. nos. *a*: FV 21; *b*: FP 24, 25; *c*: FP 14; *d*: FP 12.

Fragment *a*: R. Pococke, *Tours in Scotland 1747, 1750, 1760* 1887, pp. 33–4 with fig. 1; Pennant 1776, i, p. 93; ii, p. 407; Macdonald 1896, p. 122, fig. 5; Robertson 1975, p. 99, no. 32. Fragments *b* and *c*: Anderson 1896, p. 196, fig. 46; Robertson 1975, p. 99, no. 35. Fragment *d*: Anderson 1896, p. 197; Robertson 1975, p. 99, no. 39.

All the fragments are worn and somewhat pitted.

Fragment *a*: H.: 0.61 m.; W.: 0.68 m.; D.: 0.08 m.

Fragment *b*: H.: 0.36 m.; W.: 0.25 m.; D.: 0.075 m.

Fragment *c*: H.: 0.12 m.; W.: 0.175 m.; D.: 0.075 m.

Fragment *d*: H.: 0.16 m.; W.: 0.12 m.; D.: 0.06 m.

Relief carving. Local red sandstone.

Fragment *a* preserves the lower part of a winged female figure, evidently Victory, facing three-quarters right, with flowing draperies and left leg bare. On her feet a simple pair of sandals is held in position by thongs. Her left foot rests upon a globe, crudely marked with criss-cross bands. The bottom of the panel is bordered by a broad plain moulding, and the right and (less certainly) left sides by narrow plain mouldings. Fragments *b* and *c* preserve parts of the wing of a similar Victory figure and fragment *d* a portion of her draperies. Across the wing is the stem of a palm frond, held at breast height.

The fragments derive from a large commemorative slab, probably in three separate panels. The inscription, perhaps set within a laurel wreath, would have been flanked by winged Victory figures, each with one foot on a globe, and carrying palm branches (cf. no. 27).

Antonine date?

27   Fragments of Commemorative Slab, showing Victory Figures   PLATE 10

Prov.: Birrens (*Blatobulgium*), Dumfriesshire, during excavation of the fort-site, 1895.

Loc.: National Museum of Antiquities of Scotland, Edinburgh. Inv. nos. FP 6, 16, 7, 22.

a and *b*: Anderson 1896, p. 196, fig. 45; Robertson 1975, p. 99, nos. 33–4. *c* and *d*: EE ix, 1231a; Anderson 1896, p. 197; *RIB* 2111 (frag. *c* only) Robertson 1975, p. 98, no. 29.

The fragments are chipped and slightly worn. The left side of *b* is neatly dressed, presumably for reuse in the Roman period.

a: H.: 0.15 m.; W.: 0.18 m.; D.: 0.085 m. *b*: H.: 0.38 m.; W.: 0.36 m.; D.: 0.12 m. *c*: H.: 0.14 m.; W.: 0.2 m.; D.: 0.11 m. *d*: H.: 0.11 m.; W.: 0.14 m.; D.: 0.11 m.

Relief carving. Local red sandstone.

On *a* are the draperies of a figure moving towards the right, and on *b* the lower half of a figure, similarly draped, moving towards the left, with her left foot resting on a globe decorated with criss-cross bands. The draperies are carefully pleated, and part of an overfold is visible above. The figure wears a simple pair of sandals held in position by broad thongs. The lower margin of the slab is bordered by a wide, plain moulding.

Fragments *c* and *d* preserve segments of the left side of a laurel wreath. On *d* is a double moulding, which may be part of the upper border of the slab. Within the wreath on *c* are parts of two letters, probably AN; on *d* are serifs belonging to a single letter, perhaps M.

Enough survives to indicate that the four fragments formed part of a commemorative slab similar to no. 26, on which Victory figures, presumably winged, flanked a central panel, in the form of a laurel wreath, which contained an inscription. The inscription can be restored to show a dedication to Antoninus Pius.

Antonine date?

28 Building Stone PLATE 11

Prov.: Birrens (*Blatobulgium*), Dumfriesshire, during excavation of the fort-site, 1895.

Loc.: National Museum of Antiquities of Scotland, Edinburgh. Inv. no. FP 55.

Anderson 1896, p. 197.

H.: 0.12 m.; W.: 0.47 m.; D.: 0.145 m.

Incised with a punch or similar instrument. Local red sandstone.

A *phallus* has been incised along the length of the stone.

1st/2nd century AD (probably Hadrianic-Antonine date?).

29 Fragment of Sculptured Slab PLATE 11

Prov.: Birrens (*Blatobulgium*), Dumfriesshire, during excavation of the fort-site, 1895.

Now lost (illustration from Macdonald and Barbour).

Macdonald and Barbour 1897, pl. iiiA, fig. 24.[1]

The fragment preserved part of a side-panel of a commemorative tablet.

H.: 0.66 m.; W.: 0.365 m.; D.: —.

Relief carving. Type of stone not recorded.

The panel was decorated with a *pelta*, the outlines of which were emphasized by plain narrow mouldings which also extended along the left edge of the panel and perhaps also the top and bottom margins. The horns of the *pelta* terminated in griffin-heads, between which was an elaborate fan-shaped leaf.

1st/2nd century AD (probably Hadrianic-Antonine date?).

30 Fragments of Sculptured Slab PLATE 11

Prov.: Birrens (*Blatobulgium*), Dumfriesshire, during excavation of the fort-site, 1895.

Loc.: National Museum of Antiquities of Scotland, Edinburgh. Inv. nos. FP 10, 13, 15, 22.

Anderson 1896, p. 197; Robertson 1975, p. 99, nos. 40-2.

Four fragments, here designated *a–d*, preserve parts of one or both side-panels of a commemorative slab, on which the die was flanked by *peltae*. The fragments are chipped and worn; *a* and *b* adjoin.

a and *b*: H.: 0.22 m.; W.: 0.36 m.; D.: 0.06 m. *c*: H.: 0.17 m.; W.: 0.16 m.; D.: 0.08 m. *d*: H.: 0.09 m.; W.: 0.14 m.; D.: 0.07 m.

Relief carving. Local red sandstone.

The surviving *pelta*-horn terminates in a bird-head, and the central projection in a plain boss. The four-petalled rosette on *d* may have occupied one of the four outer corners of the slab.

1st/2nd century AD (probably Hadrianic-Antonine date?).

31 Fragment of Sculptured Slab PLATE 11

Prov.: Birrens (*Blatobulgium*), Dumfriesshire; picked up on the fort-site, 1941.

Loc.: Dundee University (temporary location).

Robertson 1975, p. 97 n. 5.

The fragment, which preserves the bottom right or top left corner of a commemorative slab, is chipped and scarred, but not much worn.

[1] Not mentioned in the main excavation report (*PSAS* xxx, 1895-6, pp. 81-199), or in the text of Macdonald and Barbour, op. cit.

H.: 0.18 m.; W.: 0.2 m.; D.: 0.065 m.

Relief carving. Local red sandstone.

The horn of a *pelta* terminates in a griffin-head, with a plain moulding above.

1st/2nd century AD (probably Hadrianic-Antonine date?).

32　Fragment of Sculptured Slab　PLATE 11

Prov.: Birrens (*Blatobulgium*), Dumfriesshire, during excavation of the fort-site, 1895.

Loc.: National Museum of Antiquities of Scotland, Edinburgh. Inv. no. FP 34.

Robertson 1975, p. 99, no. 40.

The fragment preserves part of a *pelta*, with triple mouldings tapering towards a terminal, now lost.

H.: 0.066 m.; W.: 0.08 m.; D.: 0.025 m.

1st/2nd century AD (probably Hadrianic-Antonine date?).

33　Fragments of Sculptured Slab　PLATE 12

Prov.: Birrens (*Blatobulgium*), Dumfriesshire, during excavation of the fort-site, 1895.

Loc.: National Museum of Antiquities of Scotland, Edinburgh. Inv. nos. FP 17, 29, 33, 35, 36, 37, 41, 20.

Anderson 1896, p. 197; Macdonald and Barbour 1897, pl. iiiA, fig. 23 (frag. *h*); Robertson 1975, p. 99, nos. 40, 45, 47.

The fragments, here designated *a–h*, preserve small sections of the decorated margins of a sculptured slab or carved screen. All the fragments are chipped and slightly worn.

a: H.: 0.18 m.; W.: 0.15 m.; D.: 0.05 m. *b*: H.: 0.09 m.; W.: 0.13 m.; D.: 0.06 m. *c*: H.: 0.11 m.; W.: 0.12 m.; D.: 0.03 m. *d*: H.: 0.08 m.; W.: 0.05 m.; D.: 0.03 m. *e*: H.: 0.11 m.; W.: 0.05 m.; D.: 0.03 m. *f*: H.: 0.09 m.; W.: 0.05 m.; D.: 0.03 m. *g*: H.: 0.13 m.; W.: 0.1 m.; D.: 0.07. *h*: H.: 0.17 m.; W.: 0.155 m.; D.: 0.045 m.

Relief carving. Local red sandstone.

The slab was evidently framed, or its panels demarcated, by cable mouldings of varying width, sometimes accompanied by bands of leaf designs. On *a* a plain narrow moulding cuts through the cable-pattern moulding at right angles. On *b* the cable moulding sends out a branch at 45°, cutting through the inner border. Close by is an uncertain design, which may represent talons. Fragments *d*, *e*, and *f* preserve portions of the raised cable mouldings, which have flaked away from the main slab. Fragment *h* may belong to a separate panel in the form of a gabled arch.

1st/2nd century AD (probably Hadrianic-Antonine date?).

34　Fragments of Sculptured Slab　PLATE 13

Prov.: Birrens (*Blatobulgium*), Dumfriesshire, during excavation of the fort-site, 1895.

Loc.: National Museum of Antiquities of Scotland, Edinburgh. Inv. nos. FP 11, 23, 40.

Macdonald 1896, p. 197, fig. 47; Robertson 1975, p. 99, nos. 40, 43.

Four fragments are mentioned by Macdonald, but only three can now be identified among the Birrens material at the National Museum of Antiquities, here designated *a–c*. They preserve parts of the outer mouldings of a slab or screen.

a: H.: 0.15 m.; W.: 0.245 m.; D.: 0.08 m. *b*: H.: 0.15 m.; W.: 0.21 m.; D.: 0.085 m. *c*: H.: 0.085 m.; W.: 0.075 m.; D.: 0.04 m.

Relief carving. Local red sandstone.

A frieze of tendrils links and encloses petalled rosettes.

1st/2nd century AD (probably Hadrianic-Antonine date?).

35　Fragments of Sculptured Slab　PLATE 13

Prov.: Birrens (*Blatobulgium*), Dumfriesshire, before 1968.

Loc.: Dumfries Museum. Inv. no. 1968/10.

Robertson 1975, p. 99, no. 46.

The two adjoining fragments, which are chipped, scored, and rather worn, preserve one corner of a sculptured slab.

H.: 0.15 m.; W.: 0.295 m.; D.: 0.05 m.

Relief carving. Local buff sandstone.

The slab was bordered by a band of cable-patterns, the line of which terminated in, or was interrupted by, a circular disc formed by three concentric rings.

1st/2nd century AD (probably Hadrianic-Antonine date?).

36 Fragments of Sculptured Slab PLATE 13

Prov.: Birrens (*Blatobulgium*), Dumfriesshire, during excavation of the fort-site, 1895.

Loc.: National Museum of Antiquities of Scotland, Edinburgh. Inv. nos. FP 9, 21.

Robertson 1975, p. 99, no. 42.

The fragments, here designated *a* and *b*, show a complex ribbed design, perhaps from an ornamental border or from a *pelta*. They are slightly worn and chipped.

a: H.: 0.21 m.; W.: 0.26 m.; D.: 0.07 m. *b*: H.: 0.12 m.; W.: 0.1 m.; D.: 0.06 m.

Relief carving. Local red sandstone.

1st/2nd century AD (probably Hadrianic-Antonine date?).

37 Fragments of Sculptured Slab PLATE 13

Prov.: Birrens (*Blatobulgium*), Dumfriesshire, during excavation of the fort-site, 1895.

Loc.: National Museum of Antiquities of Scotland, Edinburgh. Inv. nos. FP 18, 38, 39.

Macdonald 1896, p. 197, fig. 48; Robertson 1975, p. 99, no. 44.

The fragments, here designated *a–c*, formed parts of the decorated border of a sculptured slab. All are slightly worn and scored.

a: H.: 0.085 m.; W.: 0.145 m.; D.: 0.06 m. *b*: H.: 0.1 m.; W.: 0.16 m.; D.: 0.06 m. *c*: H.: 0.08 m.; W.: 0.14 m.; D.: 0.06 m.

Relief carving. Local red sandstone.

A continuous chain of guilloche ornaments can be seen on each fragment.

1st/2nd century AD (probably Hadrianic-Antonine date?).

38 Fragment of Sculptured Slab PLATE 14

Prov.: Birrens (*Blatobulgium*), during excavation of the fort-site, 1895.

Loc.: National Museum of Antiquities of Scotland, Edinburgh. Inv. no. FP 31.

Robertson 1975, p. 99, no. 42.

The fragment shows one corner of a sculptured slab.

H.: 0.15 m.; W.: 0.25 m.; D.: 0.07 m.

Relief carving. Local red sandstone.

A curious looped design, perhaps part of a *pelta*, can be discerned.

1st/2nd century AD (probably Hadrianic-Antonine date?).

39 Fragment of Sculptured Slab PLATE 14

Prov.: Birrens (*Blatobulgium*), Dumfriesshire, during excavation of the fort-site, 1895.

Loc.: National Museum of Antiquities of Scotland, Edinburgh. Inv. no. FP 28.

Robertson 1975, p. 99, no. 42.

The fragment shows plain narrow mouldings.

H.: 0.15 m.; W.: 0.13 m.; D.: 0.04 m.

Relief carving. Local red sandstone.

1st/2nd century AD (probably Hadrianic-Antonine date?).

40 Fragment of Moulded Cornice PLATE 14

Prov.: Birrens (*Blatobulgium*), Dumfriesshire, during excavation of the fort-site, 1895.

Loc.: National Museum of Antiquities of Scotland, Edinburgh. Inv. no. FP 19.

Macdonald and Barbour 1897, p. 41, pl. iiiA, fig. 20; Robertson 1975, p. 99, no. 42.

The fragment preserves part of an arched moulding. There is a deep vertical scar across the cornice mouldings. If the drawing in Macdonald and Barbour, op. cit., is an accurate representation of the fragment as found, some further damage to the chip-carvings has been sustained.

H.: 0.2 m.; W.: 0.24 m.; D.: 0.08 m.

Relief carving. Local red sandstone.

A band of chip-carvings close to the upper border constitutes the decoration.

1st/2nd century AD (probably Hadrianic-Antonine date?).

41 Building Stone PLATE 14

Prov.: Castledykes, Lanarkshire, unstratified, during excavation of the fort-site, 1950.

Loc.: Hunterian Museum, University of Glasgow. Inv. no. F.1950.35.

JRS xli, 1951, p. 120; Robertson 1964, p. 154, no. 1, pl. 6.

The front of the stone is chipped at top and bottom.

H.: 0.19 m.; W.: 0.29 m.; D.: 0.275 m.

Relief carving. Local grey sandstone.

The face of the stone has been dressed to receive an inscription. The rectangular die is bordered by a plain moulding flanked by curving incised lines which may have been intended as *ansae*. In the lower left corner an incised capricorn moves towards the left.

The capricorn testifies to building work carried out by the Second Legion at Castledykes.

Antonine date?

42 Commemorative Slab   PLATE 14

Prov.: Bothwellhaugh, Lanarkshire, in the *frigidarium* of the extra-mural bathhouse, during rescue excavation, 1975.

Loc.: Hunterian Museum, University of Glasgow. Inv. no. F.1982.8.

R. P. Wright, M. W. C. Hassall, and R. S. O. Tomlin, *Britannia* vii, 1976, p. 382, no. 15, pl. xxviiiB; L. J. F. Keppie, *GAJ* viii, 1981, pp. 72–3, no. 8, pl. 10, fig. 18.

The left-hand border and about one-third of the die are preserved.

H.: 0.412 m.; W.: 0.355 m.; D.: 0.135 m.

Letter heights: 0.05 m.

Relief carving. Local pinkish-buff sandstone.

The die was enclosed within a plain raised moulding, and flanked to the left (and presumably also to the right) by a zigzag border of chip-carved petals. Above the surviving letters of the inscription is the lower part of a figure, probably female, walking towards the right. Her scanty draperies are entwined about her right thigh. The inscription reads: (four lines lost) / *I* . . . . / *coh(ors)* . . . .

The slab presumably recorded the construction or reconstruction of the bathhouse by a cohort of auxiliaries, perhaps the garrison of Bothwellhaugh fort, but its identity is not known. The human figure could be Victory, although the arrangement of the draperies is reminiscent of Venus on no. 91 below.

Antonine date.

43 Flooring Slab   PLATE 14
                                        (Scale in inches)

Prov.: Bothwellhaugh, Lanarkshire, in the *frigi-*

darium of the extra-mural bathhouse, during rescue excavation, 1975.

Loc.: Hunterian Museum, University of Glasgow. Inv. no. F.1982.6.

G. S. Maxwell, *Britannia* vi, 1975, p. 35, fig. 6; R. Goodburn, ibid. vii, 1976, p. 304; L. J. F. Keppie and J. M. McKenzie, *Current Archaeology* 52, 1976, p. 154; L. J. F. Keppie, *GAJ* viii, p. 1981, p. 72, no. 6, pl. 11, fig. 17.

The slab is now badly fractured, and some small fragments are missing. Plate 14 shows the slab *in situ*.

H.: 1.14 m.; W.: 0.87 m.; D.: 0.14 m.

Relief carving. Local buff sandstone.

This squared flooring slab, with a centrally placed rosette of six petals encircled by a ring of chip-carving, served as a drain-cover. The slab is pierced between each pair of petals to allow water to pass into the drain below.

Antonine date.

44 Commemorative Slab   PLATE 15

Prov.: Cappuck, Roxburghshire, 1886.

Loc.: National Museum of Antiquities of Scotland, Edinburgh. Inv. no. FR 567.

W. Laidlaw, *HBNC* xii, 1887–9, p. 76, p. 191; ibid. xiv, 1892–3, p. 383 with fig.; id., *PSAS* xxxix, 1904–5, pp. 23–5, no. 4 with fig. 4; G. H. Stevenson and S. N. Miller, *PSAS* xlvi, 1911–12, p. 476, with fig. 12; *EE* ix, 1232; RCAHMS 1956, ii, p. 382, fig. 494; *RIB* 2119.

Less than half of the slab is preserved, showing the left-hand *pelta* and part of the die.

H.: 0.29 m.; W.: 0.22 m.; D.: 0.09 m.

Letter heights: 2–3: 0.047 m.

Relief carving. Local buff sandstone.

The die is enclosed within a double plain moulding; below, a leafy border can just be discerned. Immediately to the left, between the die and the *pelta*, is the pole of a military standard set into a chamfered base and decorated with a laurel wreath (shown in profile) and three embossed discs. At the top of the pole, the standard bends to the right, as though to pass along the upper margin of the slab. The *pelta* has been carved to show a double ivy leaf growing from a single stem; the horns terminate in recurved spirals, and the central projection in a double spiral. A bird, perched on the upper horn, pecks at a large flower bud. Below the lower horn a wild boar runs towards the right. The inscription reads: *L[eg(io)]* / *X[X V(aleria) V(ictrix)]* / *f[ec(it)]*.

The slab is a record of building work carried out at Cappuck by the Twentieth Legion, the presence of whose emblem allows the inscription to be restored with some confidence.

Antonine date.

45   Leg of Equestrian Statue   PLATE 15

Prov.: Milsington, Roxburghshire, *c.*12 km west of Hawick, 1820, together with a small bronze globular pedestal.

Loc.: National Museum of Antiquities of Scotland, Edinburgh. Inv. no. L.1920.1.

G. Macdonald, *JRS* xvi, 1926, pp. 7–16, pl. iv; J. Curle, *PSAS* lxvi, 1931–2, pp. 324–5 with fig. 27, p. 365, no. 21; RCAHMS 1956, i, p. 30; Toynbee 1964, p. 52.

Only the foot and lower leg survive. The straps of the sandal are partly lost, and the front half of the foot is somewhat cracked.

H.: 0.51 m.; W.: 0.33 m.; D.: 0.12 m.

Gilded bronze. Cast.

The foot is shod in a *calceus* with a thick sole, heavy heelguard, and plain uppers. It is secured by thick thongs, which cross above the instep and are tied at the ankle. A small hole at the base of the heel may have held a spur. Remnants of the lower folds of a garment can be seen at the very top of the fragment.

The leg, just over life-size, seems likely to have been hacked from an equestrian statue of an emperor or an imperial governor. Its findspot, in a remote valley away from any known site, suggests that it was loot, perhaps from a major town or fortress. Sir George Macdonald argued that it came from York or Chester and should be assigned a pre-Hadrianic date,[1] but such precision seems unjustified.

46   Altar to Apollo   PLATE 15

Prov.: Newstead (*Trimontium*), Roxburghshire, in a pit in the south Annexe, together with a rectangular

[1] See Macdonald, loc. cit.
[2] *RIB* 1725 (Great Chesters).

socketed plinth, during excavation of the fort-site, 1910.

Loc.: National Museum of Antiquities of Scotland, Edinburgh. Inv. no. FV 41.

Curle 1911, p. 143, no. 6, pl. xvii; *EE* ix, 1233; RCAHMS 1956, ii, p. 319, no. (vi), fig. 430; *RIB* 2120.

Parts of the bolsters and of the cornice mouldings are broken away. The plinth is worn and chipped. The sculptured motif on the left side of the shaft is defaced.

H.: 0.84 m.; W.: 0.37 m.; D.: 0.31 m.

Letter heights: 1–4: 0.035 m.; 5: 0.025 m. Plinth: H.: 0.29 m.; W.: 0.5 m.; D.: 0.35 m.

Relief carving. Local red sandstone.

The bolsters terminated in six-pointed incised rosettes. On the right face of the shaft is a bow; the object on the left can be tentatively identified as a quiver. The outlines of the *focus*-mount are emphasized by a plain narrow moulding with a double spiral centrally placed. The inscription reads: *Deo* / *Apollini* / *L(ucius) Maximius* / *Gaetulicus c(enturio)* / *leg(ionis)*.

The altar was erected to Apollo by L. Maximius Gaetulicus who is known[2] to have served in the Twentieth Legion, the probable garrison at Newstead in the early Antonine period.[3]

Antonine date (probably before AD 158).

47   Altar to Jupiter   PLATE 16

Prov.: Newstead (*Trimontium*), Roxburghshire, in the well of the headquarters building, during excavation of the fort-site, 1905.

Loc.: National Museum of Antiquities of Scotland, Edinburgh. Inv. no. FV 46.

J. Curle, *The Scotsman* 28 Oct. 1905, p. 9; *The Antiquary* xli, 1905, p. 469; T. Ross, *PSAN* ser. 3, ii, 1905, p. 132 with fig.; J. Curle, *SHR* iv, 1907, p. 449; id., 1911, p. 141, no. 3, pl. xvi; *EE* ix, 1235; RCAHMS 1956, ii, p. 317, no. 1, fig. 427; *RIB* 2123.

The left-hand bolster is partly broken away. The corners of the shaft and base are chipped and worn.

H.: 1.21 m.; W.: 0.48 m.; D.: 0.4 m.

[3] See I. A. Richmond, *PSAS* lxxxiv, 1949–50, pp. 19–21; RCAHMS 1956, ii, p. 315.

Letter heights: 1–5: 0.06 m.

Relief carving. Local buff sandstone.

The altar is devoid of decoration except on the front face of the capital where the bolsters terminate in six-pointed rosettes. The inscription reads: *I(ovi) O(ptimo) M(aximo)* / *C(aius) Arrius* / *Domitianus* / *c(enturio) leg(ionis) XX V(aleriae) V(ictricis)* / *v(otum) s(olvit) l(aetus) l(ibens) m(erito)*.

A detachment of this legion is generally supposed to have been at Newstead in the early Antonine period.

Antonine date (probably before AD 158).

48   Altar   PLATE 16

Prov.: Newstead (*Trimontium*), Roxburghshire, un-stratified, in the ditch of the east annexe, during excavation of the fort-site, 1909.

Loc.: National Museum of Antiquities of Scotland, Edinburgh. Inv. no. FV 39.

Curle 1911, p. 142, no. 4, pl. xviii.1; *EE* ix, p. 619 (n. to *EE* ix, 1239); RCAHMS 1956, ii, p. 318, no (iv); *RIB* 2125.

The lower part of the base is lost. The surface of the stone has flaked away in many places, especially on the front face of the capital and shaft. The inscription is almost totally gone, but the sides are sufficiently preserved for some general description of the overall decoration to be offered.

H.: 1.00 m.; W.: 0.55 m.; D.: 0.35 m.

Letter heights: *c*.0.05 m.

Relief carving. Local buff sandstone.

The bolsters terminated in six-pointed rosettes. The sides of the capital are ornamented with an elaborate chevron design. One of the lower mouldings on the right face is decorated with cable patterns, a design which is repeated on the front of the base. On the left side of the shaft is a *patera*, handle pointing upwards, and on the right side a jug. The inscription may have been arranged in nine lines, but only parts of the last four remain, to read: (6 lines lost) / ....C A. ./ .....IN .. / *c(enturio) l[eg(ionis) .....]* / *v(otum) s(olvit) l(aetus) [l(ibens) m(erito)]*.

This altar, like no. 47, may have been erected by the centurion C. Arrius Domitianus.

Antonine date.

49   Fragment of Commemorative Slab
PLATE 16

Prov.: Newstead (*Trimontium*), Roxburghshire, in the well of the headquarters building, during excavation of the fort-site, 1905.

Loc.: National Museum of Antiquities of Scotland, Edinburgh. Inv. no. FRA 1601.

Curle 1911, p. 144; RCAHMS 1956, ii, p. 319, no. (x).

The fragment, which is slightly chipped, preserves a small part of a sculptured slab, including its right-hand margin.

H.: 0.18 m.; W.: 0.145 m.; D.: 0.09 m.

Relief carving. Local pinkish-red sandstone.

A wild boar, head aggressively lowered, runs towards the left, with its hind legs partly overlying the raised right-hand border of the slab.

The appearance of the boar, emblem of the Twentieth Legion (as on nos. 50–1) confirms the presence of a detachment from that legion at Newstead.

Antonine date (probably before AD 158).

50   Building Stone   PLATE 16

Prov.: Newstead (*Trimontium*), Roxburghshire, in the make-up of a road in the south annexe, *c*.1825.

Now lost (illustration from Curle). A cast is preserved in the National Museum of Antiquities of Scotland. Inv. no. FV 24.

J. A. Smith, *PSAS* i, 1851–4, p. 29; Stuart 1852, p. 153, n. (a); Curle 1911, pp. 5, 144, pl. xviii.6; RCAHMS 1956, ii, p. 319, no. (x); Toynbee 1964, p. 144.

Part of the upper surface of the stone is broken away at the top left corner.

H.: 0.215 m.; W.: 0.37 m.; D.: (original stone) 0.185 m.

Relief carving. Type of stone not recorded.

On the front face of the stone is a wild boar walking towards the left. Parts of an outer raised moulding are visible to the left and below.

The boar-emblem provides further evidence for the presence at Newstead of a detachment of the Twentieth Legion, probably in the Antonine I phase. The carving is noticeably inferior in vigour and movement to nos. 49, 51.

Antonine date (probably before AD 158).

51 Impost Capital PLATE 17

Prov.: Newstead (*Trimontium*), Roxburghshire, in the well of the headquarters building, during excavation of the fort-site, 1905.

Loc.: National Museum of Antiquities of Scotland, Edinburgh. Inv. no. FRA 1604.

Curle 1911, p. 144; RCAHMS 1956, ii, p. 319, no. (x).

H.: 0.63 m.; W.: 0.49 m.; D.: 0.37 m.

Relief carving. Local red sandstone. In the top of the stone is a lewis-hole.

On one side of this roughly finished impost capital is a wild boar, running towards the left.

The use of the boar-emblem is further evidence for the presence at Newstead of a detachment of the Twentieth Legion, probably in the early Antonine period (cf. nos. 49–50).

Antonine date (probably before AD 158).

52 Moulded Cornices PLATE 17

Prov.: Newstead (*Trimontium*), Roxburghshire, from a souterrain close to the fort-site, 1845.

Loc.: Now lost except for one small fragment presented to the National Museum of Antiquities of Scotland, Edinburgh. Inv. no. FV 25 (illustration of complete block from Smith).

J. A. Smith, *PSAS* i, 1851–4, pp. 213–16; NMAS *Catalogue* 1863, p. 57, no. H157; Wilson 1851, p. 87; RCAHMS 1956, i, p. 321, no. 611.

Each stone (when found) H.: 0.2 m.; W.: 0.4 m.; D.: 0.68 m. Surviving fragment: H.: 0.08 m.; W.: 0.16 m.; D.: 0.1 m.

Relief carving. Local buff sandstone.

The lintels of the souterrain incorporated Roman cornices, two blocks of which were removed in 1845. Each stone was decorated with a horizontal line of cable-patterns.

Antonine date?

53 Fragment of *Aedicula*? PLATE 17

Prov.: Newstead, Roxburghshire, near the lower course of the Bogle Burn, before 1956.

Loc.: Abbey Museum, Melrose.

RCAHMS 1956, i, fig. 84; ii, pp. 319–20, no. (xi).

The fragment preserves what seems to be the gable-corner of an *aedicula* (similar to no. 12 above).

H.: 0.23 m.; W.: 0.235 m.; D.: 0.125 m.

Relief carving. Local reddish-buff sandstone.

The decoration, on one side of the fragment, consists of a branch with small delicately carved leaves on either side, pointing downwards. On the other side are traces of similar ornamentation.

1st/2nd century date.

54 Cavalry Sports Helmet and Face-mask
PLATE 17

Prov.: Newstead, Roxburghshire, in Pit xxii, along with no. 56 and other military equipment, during excavation of the south annexe of the fort, 1906.

Loc.: National Museum of Antiquities of Scotland, Edinburgh. Inv. no. FRA 121.

Curle 1911, p. 121, pp. 168–70, pls. xxvi.2, xxix; Toynbee 1962, p. 167, no. 99, pl. 104; 1964, pp. 291–2; H. R. Robinson, *The Armour of Imperial Rome* 1975, pp. 114–16, pls. 318–19; W. H. Manning, in D. E. Strong and D. Brown (eds.), *Roman Crafts* 1976, pl. 232; Clarke, Breeze, and Mackay 1980, p. 24, no. 13.

Parts of the forehead and both ears are missing, together with part of the upper lip. Sections of the back of the helmet, including both ear-guards, are likewise lost. The neck-guard is overlaid by a thin bronze strip. The mask is badly cracked in places.

H.: 0.24 m.; W.: 0.19 m.; D.: 0.24 m.

Beaten iron, once partly or wholly overlaid with silver.

Mask and helmet form a pair, though the point of junction does not survive. The face is clean-shaven and the features youthful. There are perforations for the eyes, and for the mouth, which is slightly open. The hair is elaborately curled and radiates from the crown. It is overlaid by a laurel wreath with dependent fillets. The forelocks extend over the mask, and other curls hang down in front of the left ear. The neck-guard is ornamented with chevrons and dots. Tubes for the attachment of plumes can be seen above the left ear and above the forehead. Other rings may have held streamers. Remnants of padding, perhaps woollen, survive on the inside of helmet and mask.

This, the most complete and most artistically satisfying of the Cavalry Sports helmets from Newstead, belongs to Robinson's Category C. Pit lvii at Newstead was sealed by cobbling belonging to an Antonine bathhouse, and was presumably in use during the Flavian occupation of the site. The discovery of this and nos. 55–6 helps confirm that the Flavian garrison at Newstead consisted of, or included, a cavalry regiment.[1]

Flavian date.

55   Face-mask from a Cavalry Sports Helmet

PLATE 18

Prov.: Newstead, Roxburghshire, in Pit lvii, along with other military equipment, during excavation of the west annexe, 1907.

Loc.: National Museum of Antiquities of Scotland, Edinburgh. Inv. no. FRA 123.

Curle 1911, p. 129, pp. 170–2, pl. xxx; Toynbee 1962, p. 167, no. 100, pl. 105; 1964, pp. 291–2; H. R. Robinson, *The Armour of Imperial Rome* 1975, pp. 124–5, pls. 359–60; K. A. Steer, *Scottish Art Review* x.2, 1965, p. 17 with pl.; J. Garbsch, *Römische Paraderüstungen* 1978, p. 69, no. O39; Clarke, Breeze, and Mackay 1980, p. 23, no. 12.

The mask is only lightly scratched, but shows evidence of repair on the forehead, and has some slight cracks.

H.: 0.22 m.; W.: 0.22 m.; D.: 0.17 m.

Beaten bronze.

This life-sized face-mask for attachment to a helmet (now lost), has perforations for the eyes, nostrils, and mouth which is shown partly open. The face is clean-shaven, the cheeks smooth, and the hair elaborately waved and braided, with a few locks falling in front of the ears. To either side of the cheeks and on the forehead are holes for attachment to the now missing helmet.

The mask formed the visor of a sports helmet of the type worn by auxiliary cavalry, and belongs to Robinson's 'Cavalry Sports E' category. The youthful features seem almost feminine, and Robinson suggested that they represent an Amazon. Mock battles against Amazons were part of the jousting ritual of cavalry tournaments.

Flavian date.

56   Cavalry Sports-helmet

PLATE 18

Prov.: Newstead, Roxburghshire, in Pit xxii, along with no. 54 and other military equipment, during excavation of the south annexe of the fort, 1906.

Loc.: National Museum of Antiquities of Scotland, Edinburgh. Inv. no. FRA 125.

Curle 1911, pp. 121–2, 166–8, pls. xxvi–xxviii; Toynbee 1962, p. 166, no. 98, pl. 104; 1964, pp. 191–2; H. R. Robinson, *The Armour of Imperial Rome* 1975, pp. 112–13, pls. 314–16; J. Garbsch, *Römische Paraderüstungen* 1978, p. 56, no. H2, taf. 12.2; K. A. Steer, *Scottish Art Review* x.2, 1965, pp. 16–17, with pl.; Clarke, Breeze, and Mackay 1980, p. 23, no. 11, pl. 1.

The helmet is slightly dented and cracked in places. The face-mask is lost. Remnants of a leather lining remain attached.

H.: 0.28 m.; W.: 0.24 m.; D.: 0.28 m.

Beaten brass.

The crown is elaborately decorated. Within a border of rope-patterns, a winged Cupid, naked except for bracelets on both arms, stands in a boat-shaped, two-wheeled chariot drawn towards the left by two leopards. In his left hand the Cupid holds the reins and in his right a whip with which he encourages the animals to greater efforts. Above, a similar cupid helps to guide the leopards by means of reins or streamers attached to their necks. In the background are palm fronds, star-clusters, and two cones. On the neck-guard is a punched inscription, which reads: *Uffi(....) t(urma) Ges(....)*.

The skull-piece belongs to a parade- or sports-helmet of the type worn by auxiliary cavalrymen at tournaments and special ceremonies (cf. nos. 54–5). The scene represents a chariot race, the finishing line being defined by the pair of cones. Pit xxii was in use during the later 1st century AD, and the helmet was perhaps thrown in at the time of the Roman withdrawal, c.AD 100. It belongs to Robinson's 'Cavalry Sports B' category.

Flavian date.

57   Head

PLATE 19

Prov.: Hawkshaw, Peeblesshire, during ploughing, in or before 1783.

---

[1] I. A. Richmond, *PSAS* lxxxiv, 1949–50, 21.

Loc.: National Museum of Antiquities of Scotland, Edinburgh. Inv. no. KG 4.

W. Smellie, *Account of the Institution and Progress of the Society of Antiquaries of Scotland* 1784, p. 110; J. Curle, *PSAS* lxvi, 1931–2, pp. 326–9, figs. 28 and 30, no. 37; Toynbee 1962, p. 126; 1964, p. 58; RCAHMS 1967, p. 35 with pl. 1, p. 236.

Damage has been sustained to the nose and forehead. The ears are slightly chipped and the lower part of the head, below the mouth, has been broken away. The back of the head is only roughly worked.

H.: 0.27 m.; W.: 0.24 m.; D.: 0.25 m.

Carved in the round. Cream marble.

The head, a little larger than life-size, is the portrait of a middle-aged man. The mouth has a pronounced downward curve at the corners, and the musculature of the cheeks is loose. The hair is combed forward from the crown and over the forehead. The lack of attention paid to the back of the head suggests that it was intended to be displayed in a niche.

The hair-style is characteristic of male portraiture in the latter part of Trajan's reign. Although the size of the head indicates that it represented someone of importance, the features do not closely resemble those of recognized portraits of the emperor; J. M. C. Toynbee has suggested that it may be the portrait of a general or a provincial governor. Most commentators have seen the influence of Gaulish sculpture in the rigid patterning of the hair. The findspot, well away from a Roman site, suggests that the head may have arrived in Scotland as loot from the south.

Trajanic date.

58 Building Stone PLATE 19

Prov.: Built into a souterrain at Crichton Mains, Midlothian; first seen, 1869.

Loc.: *In situ* (illustration from Edwards; cast in National Museum of Antiquities of Scotland, Edinburgh. Inv. no. FR 441).

A. J. H. Edwards, *PSAS* lix, 1924–5, pp. 94–5; RCAHMS 1929, pp. 53–4.

The slab (to judge from the cast) was slightly worn.

Dimensions of cast: H.: 0.125 m.; W.: 0.195 m.

Relief carving. Local sandstone.

The front face of this stone is carved to show the head, wings, and fore-parts of a pegasus, flying towards the right.[1]

The pegasus, one of the emblems of the Second Legion, indicates building work by the legion or a detachment. The Crichton souterrain incorporates other Roman building stones, so that the presence nearby of a fort or fortlet on the line of Dere Street can be assumed.

Antonine date?

59 Pine-cone Finial PLATE 19

Prov.: Midfield Mains, Midlothian, in a ditch with associated Roman finds, 1 km south-east of Inveresk fort, 1879.

Loc.: National Museum of Antiquities of Scotland, Edinburgh. Inv. no. FV 31.

PSAS xiii, 1878–9, pp. 267–8, with fig.: W. Stevenson, ibid., pp. 271–2; RCAHMS 1929, p. 93.

The cone was broken into two pieces at the time of discovery, but repaired.

H.: 0.5 m.; W.: 0.28 m.; D.: 0.21 m.

Carved in the round. Local buff sandstone.

The finial, which probably came from a gravestone or tomb-monument, was carved in the form of a pine-cone, a symbol of life after death.

Antonine date?

60 Pilaster Capital PLATE 19

Prov.: Inveresk, Midlothian, on the fort-site, 1946, together with two fragments of shaft, and a column base.

Loc.: National Museum of Antiquities of Scotland, Edinburgh. Inv. no. FR 782(d).

PSAS ci, 1968–9, p. 293 with fig. 4; G. S. Maxwell, *PSAS* cxiii, 1983, forthcoming.

One corner of the capital has been broken away, probably at the moment of discovery.

Dimensions of capital: H.: 0.28 m.; W.: 0.18 m.; D.: 0.23 m. Total length of surviving column: 0.29 m.

Carved in the round. Local orange-buff sandstone, with a whitish surface.

The capital is decorated with upright leaves, in imitation of the Corinthian style. Above, are incised

[1] Cf. Phillips 1977, no. 168.

saltire crosses. The pilaster is finished off on two sides only and was evidently meant to stand at one side of a porch or entrance-way.

Antonine date?

61 Relief of Three Mother Goddesses

PLATE 19

Prov.: Unknown, but first reported built into a garden wall at Hailes House, Colinton, Midlothian, 1917.

Loc.: The Abbey, Fort Augustus, Inverness-shire (fibreglass cast in National Museum of Antiquities of Scotland, Edinburgh. Inv. no. FV 61).

G. Macdonald, *PSAS* lii, 1917–18, pp. 38–48; RCAHMS 1929, p. 17, fig. 19, no. 24.

The stone is weathered. The head of the right-hand figure and the shell canopy above it are missing. The heads of the other figures are so badly worn that no details remain.

H.: 0.47 m.; W.: 0.52 m.; D.: —.

Relief carving. Local buff sandstone.

The three mother goddesses sit shoulder to shoulder, apparently on the same bench, beneath a canopy which originally consisted of three fluted shells: between the two surviving shells is a circular boss. At the bottom right is the lower part of a column which once supported the canopy.

The goddesses are identically dressed in long robes with fine, stylized folds. Each wears a shawl which is tightly drawn across her shoulders and upper arms, and fastened centrally with a large, circular brooch. From the outlines of the surviving heads, it appears either that the goddesses wore headdresses which were bulky and included some covering for the neck,[1] or that the heads were disproportionately large and the necks very thick.[2]

Each goddess holds a round fruit in one hand. The figure on the left carries a wicker basket full of corn. The goddess on the right grasps both her fruit and the handle of a square basket in her left hand, while her right hand lies, apparently empty, across her breast. The central figure holds a large bunch of grapes which spills over the edge of her lap and falls almost to her feet.

This relief is the only representation of the *Matres* reported from Scotland. The sculptor, or his patron, must have had in mind deities from an area where the grape was an important local product, but, although grapes can be distinguished among the contents of cornucopiae or baskets carried by several mother goddesses from Gaul and the Rhineland, the bunch of grapes held by the central figure on the Colinton relief seems to be unique. The triple shell-canopy is also unusual, although a number of mother goddesses from Germany, Gaul, and Britain are portrayed beneath single shells. A relief showing a man sacrificing at an altar before the statues of three mother goddesses, each seated within her own shell-canopied niche, comes from Carlisle in Cumbria.[3]

2nd/3rd century AD date?

62 Altar to Neptune

PLATE 20

Prov.: Cramond, Midlothian, before 1732.

Loc.: Now lost. Last seen at Neidpath Castle, Peebles, in 1794 (illustration from Horsley).

Horsley 1732, p. 204, pl. (*Scotland*) xxviii; Wood 1794, p. 9, fig. iv; Wilson 1851, p. 391; Stuart 1852, p. 170; S. Lysons, *Archaeologia* xviii, 1815, p. 120, pl. vii.2; RCAHMS 1929, p. 41; Ross 1967, p. 142.

Only the upper part of the altar survived. Horsley's drawing shows the capital and part of the shaft.

No measurements given.

Relief carving. Red sandstone.

On one side of the capital was a horned, bearded head, facing front. From beneath the beard protruded two bulbous, tapering objects. Comparison with a closely similar head on a mosaic pavement from Withington in Gloucestershire shows that these objects were intended to represent dolphins and that the head was that of the god Neptune with lobster-claws in his hair rather than a Celtic deity (e.g. Cernunnos) with antler-horns.[4]

2nd/3rd century AD date?

---

[1] Macdonald, loc. cit., suggests that they may have worn pointed hoods. Mother goddesses wearing coifs come from Gaul (e.g. Espérandieu. 1374, 6774 = 7799), from Caerwent, Monmouthshire (V. E. Nash-Williams, *BBCS* xv, 1954, pp. 88–9, pl. vi), and from Newcastle upon Tyne (Phillips 1977, no. 236, pl. 63).

[2] Cf. a trio of mother goddesses from Ashcroft in Cirencester, Gloucestershire (Toynbee 1964, p. 172, pl. xliii).

[3] See R. P. Wright and E. J. Phillips, *Roman Inscribed and Sculptured Stones in Carlisle Museum* 1975, no. 187.

[4] S. Lysons, loc. cit.

63 Altar?

Prov.: Cramond, Midlothian, before 1786.

Now lost.

James Douglas, Earl of Morton, *Ancient Inscriptions on Stones found in Scotland* (MS formerly in the Library of the Society of Antiquaries of Scotland; not now traceable), before 1786, p. 7; Wilson 1851, p. 392; *CIL* vii, 1087; RCAHMS 1929, p. 41; *RIB* 2136.

H.: 0.915 m.; W.: 0.45 m.; D.: —.

Relief carving. Type of stone not recorded.

Morton reports an inscribed slab, 'having four lyons drawn on it, all being almost worn out'. The inscription read: *C(aius) Publius Cr[...]/[....] in Pomponian[.. / ....] / p[r]a[e]f(ectus) p(osuit) d(edit) d(edicavit).*

2nd/3rd century AD date?

64 Sculptured Slab

Prov.: Cramond, Midlothian, in the garden of the manse, 1745.

Now lost.

Wood 1794, p. 11; RCAHMS 1929, p. 39.

'About 18" square.'

Relief carving. Type of stone not recorded.

The slab showed an eagle grasping lightning in its talons.

2nd/3rd century AD date?

65 Sculptured Relief of a Genius? PLATE 20

Prov.: Eagle Rock, West Lothian, on the foreshore of the River Forth, about 0.5 km west of the fort-site at Cramond.

Loc.: *In situ.*

Wood 1794, p. 12; Stuart 1852, p. 17 n.; RCAHMS 1929, p. xxxiii, no. 330, p. 208; D. J. Breeze, *Roman Scotland, A Guide to the Visible Remains* 1979, p. 39.

The figure is badly worn.

Dimensions of niche: H.: 0.85 m.; W.: 0.73 m.; D.: 0.25 m.

Relief carving. Local buff sandstone.

The near vertical east face of the rock has been carved to show an upright figure within a niche, below which is a rectangular panel which may once have borne (or have been intended to bear) an inscription. The figure has traditionally been identified as an eagle (hence the modern name of the rock itself). It seems, rather, to show a Genius wearing a mural crown, and holding a cornucopia in the crook of his left arm. In his right hand he holds a *patera*, over an altar.[1]

2nd–3rd century AD date?

66 Milestone PLATE 20

Prov.: Ingliston, West Lothian, before 1697.

Loc.: National Museum of Antiquities of Scotland, Edinburgh. Inv. nos. FV 29, 30.

Sibbald 1697, p. 206; 1707, p. 50; W. Camden, *Britannia*, ed. E. Gibson, 1722, p. 1189; Gordon 1726, p. 62, pl. xii.3; Horsley 1732, *praef.* p. xii, p. 203, pl. (*Scotland*) xxv; Hodgson 1840, p. 263, no. cclx; Stuart 1852, p. 170; *CIL* vii, 1085; *EE* ix, p. 620; RCAHMS 1929, p. 40; I. A. Richmond, *Northumberland County History* xv, 1940, p. 76, no. 4; *RIB* 2313; E. B. Birley, *JRS* lvi, 1966, p. 230; E. A. Cormack, *PSAS* ci, 1968-9, pp. 290-1; R. P. Wright and M. W. C. Hassall, *Britannia* iv, 1973, pp. 336-7; *AE* 1975, 581; G. S. Maxwell, *PSAS* cxiii, 1983, forthcoming.

The upper half of a milestone is preserved in two adjoining fragments, which are badly worn and considerably damaged near the join. The upper fragment, which for many years was believed lost, was relocated in the store of the National Museum of Antiquities, Edinburgh, in 1972. Two lines of the inscription were erased in antiquity.

H.: 1.1 m.; Diam.: 0.39 m.

Letter heights: 2-3: 0.06 m.; 6-7: 0.045-0.06 m.

Relief carving. Local buff sandstone.

Below a circular wreath with two dependent fillets is an inscription contained within a frame bordered by plain mouldings and flanked by two small ansate panels. The inscription reads: *I[mp(eratori) Caes(ari) T(ito) | Ael(io) Hadr(iano) Anto]/n[i]no Aug(usto) Pio/p(atri) p(atriae) co(n)s(ul) [I]II/.............../ ..../ [co]h(ors) I Cugernor(um) | [Tri]monti(o) m(ilia) p(assuum) | [...........*

---

[1] The identification of the figure as Mercury (RCAHMS, loc. cit.), holding a *caduceus* in his left hand, is in our view less likely.

With the rediscovery of the upper section, the milestone can be seen to have commemorated the building or refurbishment, by the First Cohort of *Cugerni*, of a road from Newstead (*Trimontium*) to the river Forth, at the beginning of the Antonine period of occupation (rather than in the Severan period, as hitherto frequently averred). The two lines of the inscription which have been erased probably carried the name of the then governor of the province of Britain: he is unlikely to have been Lollius Urbicus (as R. W. Davies has suggested)[1] but very probably his immediate successor, whose name is not known.[2]

AD 140–4.[3]

[1] *Chiron* vii, 1977, pp. 390–2.
[2] A. R. Birley, *The Fasti of Roman Britain* 1981, pp. 115–16.
[3] For a discussion of the date, which depends on whether COS II or COS III is the preferred reading in line 4, see Maxwell, loc. cit. Also reported at Ingliston is a sculptured panel showing a bird of uncertain species in high relief, standing with wings fully outstretched; see E. A. Cormack, *PSAS* ci, 1968–9, p. 291. This panel has no connection with the milestone and its date must remain uncertain. Now in the possession of Dr Cormack.

PART II

THE ANTONINE WALL

THE ANTONINE WALL

67   Centurial Stone   PLATE 21

Prov.: Carriden (*Veluniate*), West Lothian. Seen built into a wall of Carriden House, *c*.1725.

Now lost (illustration from Horsley. The version offered by Gordon differs slightly).

Gordon 1726, p. 60, pl. x.6; Horsley 1732, p. 202, pl. (*Scotland*) xxiv; Sibbald 1707, p. 30; Stuart 1852, p. 362, pl. xv.i; *CIL* vii, 1089; A. Gibb, *Scottish Antiquary* xv, 1901, pp. 16-19, 130; F. J. Haverfield, *PSAS* xliv, 1909-10, p. 321; RCAHMS 1929, p. 198; Macdonald 1934, p. 191; *RIB* 2138.

No measurements given.

Relief carving. Type of stone not recorded.

The front of this oblong building stone showed a central panel flanked by *ansae*, each containing a roundel. In Horsley's drawing, vertical cable-mouldings separate the die from the *ansae*. The inscription, occupying the left half of the die, read: *coh*(*ortis*) | *VIII* | *c*(*enturia*) *Sta*(*tili*) | *Teles*(*phori*). To the right an eagle perched on a thunderbolt, its wings outstretched and its head turned to face the inscription, holds a wreath in its beak. On either side of the eagle is a military standard.

   Antonine date?

68   Distance Slab of the Second Legion
                                         PLATE 21

Prov.: Bridgeness, West Lothian, at the presumed eastern terminus of the Antonine Wall, 1868.

Loc.: National Museum of Antiquities of Scotland, Edinburgh. Inv. no. FV 27.

C. Roach Smith, *Gent. Mag.* N.S. iii.5, 1868, p. 763; J. H. Lefroy, *Arch. J.* xxvi, 1869, pp. 178-9; H. Cadell, *PSAS* viii, 1868-9, pp. 109-10 with pl.; J. C. Bruce, *Trans. Glasgow Arch. Soc.* 1867-83, pp. 66-70; *CIL* vii, 1088; A. Gibb, *Scottish Antiquary* xiv, 1900, pp. 181-2; ibid. xv, 1901, pp. 19-25; F. J. Haverfield and H. S. Jones, *JRS* ii, 1912, pp. 128-30, fig. 9;

RCAHMS 1929, p. 197, no. 306, fig. 18; Macdonald 1934, p. 362, no. 1, pls. iii.2, lxi; Toynbee 1962, p. 166, no. 97, pl. 102; 1964, pp. 148-9; *RIB* 2139, pl. xviii; E. J. Phillips, *PSAS* cv, 1972-4, pp. 176-82, pl. 9; H. R. Robinson, *The Armour of Imperial Rome* 1975, pl. 308; Keppie 1979, p. 9, no. 1; Clarke, Breeze, and Mackay 1980, pp. 14-15 with pl. and fig.; J. Close-Brooks, *PSAS* cxi, 1981, pp. 519-20.

The slab is fractured diagonally across the die. The top right-hand corner has been broken off, but is preserved except for one triangular segment. The sculptured figures are damaged in the vicinity of the break. During restoration work in 1978, it was discovered that one small fragment had been wrongly positioned when the slab was first reassembled in the nineteenth century. The fragment has been re-aligned, but has not added to our knowledge of the scene.

H.: 0.88 m.; W.: 2.794 m.; D.: 0.2 m.

Letter heights: lines 1-4: 0.08 m.; line 5: 0.07 m.

Relief carving. Local greyish-buff sandstone. Triangular cramp-holes have been recessed into the top and side faces of the slab. Traces of the original red paint in the letters and on the sculptured scenes were observed during cleaning in 1978.

   The die is enclosed by plain mouldings and flanked by *peltae*, the horns and central projections of which terminate in griffin-heads facing inwards towards the die. Above and below the *peltae* are six-petalled rosettes. The die is demarcated from the sculptured panels to left and right by columns: that on the left has a plain capital and base and a spiralled shaft; that on the right is all but concealed behind the frame of the adjacent scene.[1]

   To the left, under a low archway, a cavalryman, presumably an *eques legionis*, in leather cuirass, helmet with streaming crest, and a cloak which billows out behind, appears to gallop over four naked warriors. His spear is poised to strike. In his left hand

---

[1] For a detailed study of the slab, drawing attention to the lack of symmetry, and other imperfections in its execution, see E. J. Phillips, loc. cit.

is an oval shield with a raised circular boss, and at his right side a sword suspended from a baldric. His horse rears up on its hind legs, its nostrils flaring. Its tail is carefully bound and the details of its trappings can be clearly made out. One native, who has dropped his sword, holds up his rectangular shield to protect himself against the cavalryman's onslaught; a second native falls forward, with a spear-shaft protruding from his back; a third, decapitated, sits with his back to the spectator. He grasps a spear horizontally in his hands.[1] The severed head lies to the right. A fourth native, perhaps stunned by the onslaught, or resigned to his fate, sits cradling his chin in his hand. A second shield and a dagger lie on the ground nearby.

The scene to the right depicts a sacrifice. Within a gabled archway, four men, in tunics and military cloaks, look on while a *toga*-clad figure with a *patera* in his right hand sacrifices at an altar.[2] Above the group is a *vexillum*, inscribed *leg(io) II Aug(usta)*. To the right of the altar is a flute player (*tubicen*), with the double-pipes to his lips. Below him three animals, a pig, a sheep, and a bull, advance towards the altar. A small figure, half-kneeling, half-sitting, appears to beckon to them; his cloak is fastened by a large brooch at his right shoulder. He can be identified as the *victimarius*. The inscription reads: *Imp(eratori) Caes(ari) Tito Aelio | Hadri(ano) Antonino | Aug(usto) Pio p(atri) p(atriae) leg(io) II | Aug(usta) per m(ilia) p(assuum) IIIIDCLII | fec(it)*.

The slab commemorates the completion of 4652 paces of the Antonine Wall, probably from the Bridgeness promontory to Inveravon, by the Second Legion *Augusta*. It is the largest known of the distance slabs, and its findspot presumably marks the starting point of the Wall at Bridgeness. The scene on the left symbolizes Roman victories over the local tribesmen; the sacrifice on the right can be identified as a *suovetaurilia*, a ritual cleansing of the officers and men of the legion in preparation for the tasks ahead.[3]

Antonine date (probably AD 142–3).

69   Fragment of a Statue   PLATE 22

Prov.: Mumrills, Stirlingshire, during excavation of the fort-site, 1923–8.

Loc.: National Museum of Antiquities of Scotland, Edinburgh. Inv. no. FR 543.

Unpublished.

The fragment, which is chipped and worn, preserves part of a helmet-plume.

H.: 0.95 m.; W.: 0.17 m.; D.: 0.065 m.

Carved in the round. Local buff sandstone.

The fragment presumably belonged to a statue in military dress, perhaps Mars.

Antonine date.

70   Fragment of Statue   PLATE 22

Prov.: Mumrills, Stirlingshire, during excavation of the fort-site, 1923–8.

Loc.: National Museum of Antiquities of Scotland, Edinburgh. Inv. no. FRB 593.

Macdonald and Curle 1929, p. 566, fig. 129.

The fragment, which is slightly chipped, preserves the neck and part of the torso of a small statue.

H.: 0.12 m.; W.: 0.1 m.; D.: 0.04 m.

Round the neck are two bands of decoration: an upper collar decorated with diamond-patterns, and a lower ornamented with raised circular studs. Below, the folds of an outer garment meet to left of centre.

Antonine date.

71   Fragment of Sculptured Slab   PLATE 22

Prov.: First reported built into a roadside wall near Laurieston, Stirlingshire, 400 m south-east of Mumrills fort, c.1923.

Loc.: Falkirk Museum, to which it was transferred in 1935.[4]

Macdonald and Curle 1929, p. 566, fig. 130.

The fragment, which preserves the bottom-left corner of a sculptured slab or screen, is worn and blackened, perhaps by burning.

H.: 0.37 m.; W.: 0.215 m.; D.: 0.13 m.

Relief carving. Local buff sandstone.

A vertical branch sends out leaves to left and right.

[1] The third native is normally described as facing the front, with hands bound behind his back, a motif used several times on distance slabs (cf. nos. 84, 149). But a vertical incision appears to indicate his spine, and the left thigh is seen from behind.

[2] Identified by J. C. Bruce, loc. cit. as Lollius Urbicus, but no

particular individual may be intended.

[3] See I. S. Ryberg, *The Rites of the State Religion in Roman Art* 1955, pp. 104–19.

[4] Information from Mrs J. F. Murray, who cites a letter of February 1935 suggesting its removal to the safekeeping of the Museum.

Near the bottom of the branch are round bosses, possibly rosettes. To the left and below, the fragment is bordered by a plain raised moulding.

Antonine date.

72 Fragment of Commemorative Slab PLATE 22

Prov.: First reported at Callendar House, Falkirk, 1797.[1]
Loc.: Abbotsford House, Melrose, Roxburghshire, built into a garden wall.

J. Wilson, in Sir J. Sinclair (ed.), *The Statistical Account of Scotland* xix, 1797, p. 110; *CIL* vii, 846 with *Addit.* p. 310; J. C. Bruce, *Lapidarium Septentrionale* 1875, no. 804; *EE* iii, p. 136, ix, pp. 601, 623; F. J. Haverfield, *CW* ser. 2, xiii, 1913, p. 193, no. 25; E. Ritterling, *RE* xii.2, 1925, cols. 1812–13; Macdonald 1934, p. 406 n. 3; RCAHMS 1956, ii, p. 301, no. (19); *RIB* 2216; L. J. F. Keppie, *Britannia* xii, 1982, p. 100.

Only the left half of the die is preserved, flanked by an ansate panel.

H.: 0.61 m.; W.: 0.63 m.; D.: —.
Letter heights: 1–3: 0.08 m.
Relief carving. Local buff sandstone.

Above the *ansa* are the forelegs of an animal, possibly a capricorn, the emblem of the Twenty-second Legion. The inscription reads: *Vexi*[*llatio*] | *leg*(*ionis*) *XXI*[*I*] | *Primig*[*eniae*].

The slab records construction work by the Twenty-second Legion, *Primigenia*, which formed the garrison at Mainz in Upper Germany during the Antonine period. The legion is known to have sent a detachment to Britain under Hadrian.[2] If genuinely ascribed to the Falkirk area, the slab may commemorate building work at the as yet unlocated Falkirk fort, or on the Antonine Wall.[3]

Antonine date?

73 Shoulder of a Statue PLATE 22

Prov.: Rough Castle, Stirlingshire, during excavation of the fort-site, 1903.

Loc.: National Museum of Antiquities of Scotland, Edinburgh. Inv. no. FR 366.

Anderson 1905, p. 497 with fig. 5; Macdonald 1934, p. 445, fig. 54.

The fragment, which is rather worn, preserves the back portion of the left shoulder and part of the upper arm of a statue, about two-thirds life-size. The front has been sheared off vertically.

H.: 0.4 m.; W.: 0.19 m.; D.: 0.12 m.
Carved in the round. Local buff sandstone.

Below the folds of a heavy cloak is the sleeve of a tunic, elaborately frilled and fringed. The statue, of a figure in military dress, probably represented the god Mars.

Antonine date.

74 Cornice Mouldings PLATE 22

Prov.: Rough Castle, Stirlingshire, during excavation of the fort-site, 1903.

Loc.: National Museum of Antiquities of Scotland, Edinburgh. Inv. no. FR 367.

Anderson 1905, p. 497.

The two adjoining fragments preserve parts of the mouldings from the base or capital of an altar.

H.: 0.05 m.; W.: 0.155 m.; D.: 0.02 m.
Relief carving. Local rusty-buff sandstone.

Running along the length of the surviving fragments is a single line of cable-patterns.

Antonine date.

75 Fragment of Sculptured Slab PLATE 23

Prov.: Rough Castle, Stirlingshire, during excavation of the fort-site, 1903.

Loc.: National Museum of Antiquities of Scotland, Edinburgh. Inv. no. FR 368.

Anderson 1905, p. 497.

The fragment has flaked off a sandstone slab.

H.: 0.12 m.; W.: 0.75 m.; D.: 0.02 m.
Relief carving. Local reddish-buff sandstone.

---

[1] For a discussion of the provenance of the stone, which has been assigned by some scholars, on the authority of J. C. Bruce, to Old Penrith, see R. P. Wright, on *RIB* 2216.

[2] *CIL* x, 5829 = *ILS* 2726, with M. G. Jarrett, *Britannia* vii, 1976, pp. 145–7.

[3] The three British legions received reinforcement from both German provinces in AD 158 (see *RIB* 1322). For reinforcement from the same source in the early third century AD, see E. B. Birley, *Epigr. Stud.* iv, 1967, pp. 103–7.

To the right is a leaf with a central stem, and, to the left, the edge of a second leaf.

Antonine date.

76   Relief of Fortuna   PLATE 23

Prov.: Castlecary, Stirlingshire, in a niche in one of the rooms of the fort bathhouse, close to an altar to Fortuna (*RIB* 2146), 1771.

Loc.: Hunterian Museum, University of Glasgow. Inv. no. F.43.

University of Glasgow 1768 (*Suppl. c.*1771), pl. xxix; Roy 1793, App. 4 by J. Anderson (dated 1773), p. 201; Stuart 1852, pp. 345-6, pl. xiv.8; Macdonald 1897, p. 90, no. 40, pl. xi.1; Macdonald 1934, p. 446, pl. lxxvii.1; RCAHMS 1963, p. 105, no. (i), pl. 9D.; Toynbee 1964, p. 164.

The surface of the stone is chipped and worn, and a small portion of the outer moulding is broken away at the top right corner.

H.: 0.39 m.; W.: 0.25 m.; D.: 0.12 m.

Relief carving. Local buff sandstone.

Within a niche topped by a low arch, Fortuna stands facing the front. She is clad in a *toga*-like gown, with stylized diagonal folds, leaving the right shoulder bare. Her hair is cut very short, or perhaps pinned up at the back. In her left hand she holds a tall cornucopia, which rests against her upper arm. Her right hand supports a rudder, below which is a six-spoked wheel.

Fortuna, who offered protection from harm and good fortune in war, was frequently worshipped in military bathhouses in the North.[1] The cornucopia, rudder, and wheel are her familiar attributes. The carving is extremely naïve: the sculptor was, it seems, trying to show the goddess with her weight on her right leg, but the result is a badly proportioned figure whose body is out of alignment with the head and shoulders.

Antonine date.

77   Altar to Neptune   PLATE 23

Prov.: Castlecary, Stirlingshire, to the west of the fort-site, near the Red Burn, before 1845.

Loc.: National Museum of Antiquities of Scotland, Edinburgh. Inv. no. FV 33.

Stuart 1852, p. 350, pl. xiv.2; F. J. Haverfield, *Arch. J.* l, 1893, p. 304, no. 160; *CIL* vii, 1096; *EE* ix, p. 624; Macdonald 1934, pp. 421-2, no. 37; G. Macdonald, *PSAS* lvii, 1922-3, p. 175 n. 2; RCAHMS 1963, i, p. 105, no. (iii); *RIB* 2149; R. W. Davies, *PSAS* cviii, 1976-7, pp. 168-73.

The surface of the stone is badly weathered and chipped in places. The upper part of the inscription is almost illegible.

H.: 0.95 m.; W.: 0.335 m.; D.: 0.29 m.

Letter heights: 1-9: 0.03-0.035 m.

Relief carving. Local buff sandstone.

The bolsters are decorated with crudely incised rosettes. Below the *focus*-mount is a recessed scallop shell. The back and sides of the altar are plain. The inscription reads: *Deo | Neptuno | cohors I | Fid(a) Vardul(lorum) | c(ivium) R(omanorum) eq(uitata) m(illiaria) | cui pra(e)est | Trebius | Verus pr|aef(ectus)*.

The altar was dedicated to Neptune by a prefect of the First Cohort of *Vardulli*, Trebius Verus, who is also attested in this command on a diploma from Colchester.[2]

Antonine date.

78   Sculptured Panel   PLATE 23

Prov.: Castlecary, Stirlingshire, during the construction of the Glasgow to Edinburgh railway, 1841.

Loc.: National Museum of Antiquities of Scotland, Edinburgh. Inv. no. FV 35.

Stuart 1852, p. 351, pl. xiv.11; Macdonald 1934, p. 448; RCAHMS 1963, i, p. 106, no. (xi).

The slab is much weathered, and chipped round the edges.

H.: 0.235 m.; W.: 0.69 m.; D.: 0.14 m.

Relief carving. Local buff sandstone.

Within a plain raised moulding is a hunting scene in a woodland setting. Two stags stand with horns locked. To the left, a small human figure with bow at the ready advances through the trees unobserved by the animals who are preoccupied with their struggle. The figure is clad in a pointed cap, a tunic to the knee, and

---

[1] See I. A. Richmond, *AA* ser. 4, xxi, 1943, pp. 213-14; Phillips 1977, no. 183 for a similar figure at Corbridge; also below, no. 139.
[2] *CIL* xvi, 130.

a short cloak billowing out behind. On the right, a second figure stands facing the front, with a spear upright in his left hand.

The panel perhaps decorated a shrine in close proximity to the fort-site. The two human figures have been identified as Diana and Apollo, but are more likely to represent local deities of the woodland.[1]

Antonine date.

79 Leg of Statue PLATE 23

Prov.: Castlecary, Stirlingshire, before 1851.

Loc.: National Museum of Antiquities of Scotland, Edinburgh. Inv. no. FV 18.

NMAS *Catalogue* 1863, p. 56, no. H146; Macdonald 1934, p. 445; RCAHMS 1963, i, p. 106, no. (xii).

The fragment preserves the right knee and thigh of a statue of about one-third life-size.

H.: 0.15 m.; W.: 0.05–0.06 m.; D.: 0.55–0.75 m.

Carved in the round. Creamy white marble.

Antonine date.

80 Commemorative Slab PLATE 23

Prov.: Castlecary, Stirlingshire, 1764.

Loc.: Hunterian Museum, University of Glasgow. Inv. no. F.20.

University of Glasgow 1768 (*Suppl. c.*1771), pl. xxvii; Roy 1793, App. no. 4 by J. Anderson (dated 1773), p. 200, pl. xxxix; Gough 1806, iv, p. 102; Hodgson 1840, p. 265, no. cclxiv; Stuart 1852, p. 347, pl. xv.10; *CIL* vii, 1099; Macdonald 1897, p. 72, no. 29, pl. xi; Macdonald 1934, p. 412, no. 30, pl. iii; *RIB* 2155; RCAHMS 1963, i, pp. 105–6, no. (iv).

The surface of the slab is much pitted, and parts of the upper and lower mouldings of the die are broken away.

Relief carving. Local buff sandstone.

H.: 0.55 m.; W.: 1.065 m.; D.: 0.15 m.

Letter heights: 1–4: 0.06 m.

The die is bordered by a triple moulding, and flanked by hollowed-out *peltae*, whose horns and central projections terminate in large plain bosses. The inscription reads: *Imp(eratori) Caes(ari) T(ito) Ael(io) Ant(onino) | Aug(usto) Pio p(atri) p(atriae) | coh(ors) I Tungro/rum fecit m(illiaria)*.

The slab commemorates construction work by the First Cohort of *Tungri* at Castlecary fort. The ∞ sign was at one time interpreted to mean that this cohort was responsible for the building of a short length of 1000 *passus* of the Antonine Wall in the vicinity of Castlecary,[2] but the sign is almost certainly an abbreviation for *milliaria*, indicating the numerical strength of the cohort.[3]

Antonine date.

81 Centurial Stone PLATE 24

Prov.: Castlecary, Stirlingshire, during the construction of the Glasgow to Edinburgh railway, 1841.

Loc.: National Museum of Antiquities of Scotland, Edinburgh. Inv. no. FV 17.

Wilson 1851, p. 401; Stuart 1852, p. 348, pl. xiv.1; *CIL* vii, 1100; Macdonald 1934, p. 401, pl. lxxii; RCAHMS 1963, i, p. 106, no. (v); *RIB* 2156.

The stone is chipped and weathered, especially at the corners.

H.: 0.307 m.; W.: 0.38 m.; D.: 0.12 m.

Letter heights: 1–2: 0.03 m.; 3: 0.035 m.

Relief carving. Local buff sandstone.

Into the front of this squared-off building stone is recessed an ansate panel, bearing the inscription: *c(o)ho(rtis) VI | c(enturia) Anto(ni) | Arati*. Between lines 2 and 3 of the inscription are two sets of oblique parallel dashes. Above, two incised ivy leaves, of differing lengths, sprout from the top corners of the panel. In the upper angles between the *ansae* and the central panel are incised palm branches.

The stone testifies to work carried out at Castlecary by a century of legionaries.

Antonine date.

82 Building Stone PLATE 24

Prov.: First seen built into the west wall of the garden at Castlecary Castle, Stirlingshire; presumably from the nearby fort-site.

---

[1] An archer in similar attire is shown in pursuit of deer on a stone from Jarrow; see Phillips 1977, no. 329. An altar from Risingham depicts the Celtic god Cocidius as an archer in short tunic (Phillips 1977, no. 234).

[2] So E. Hübner, on *CIL* vii, 1099.
[3] R. P. Wright, on *RIB* 2155. Cf. R. W. Davies, *Epigr. Stud.* 4, 1967, p. 110.

Loc.: Castlecary Castle.

RCAHMS 1963, i, p. 106, no. (xiii).

Worn by exposure to the elements.

H.: 0.325 m.; W.: 0.45 m.; D.: —.

Relief carving. Local buff sandstone.

A *phallus* is carved lengthwise on the stone, with oblique lines running from it towards the top left and lower left corners of the stone.

    Antonine date.

83   Head

Prov.: Near Cumbernauld, Dunbartonshire, 'dug out of the Wall', 1752.

Now lost.

Scots Magazine xiv, 1752, p. 508; Stuart 1852, p. 345 n. (b).

No measurements given.

Carved in the round? Type of stone not recorded.

A head 'curiously cut out of stone' is reported.

    Antonine date?

84   Two Fragments of a Distance Slab?

                               PLATE 24

Prov.: Hag Knowe, Dunbartonshire, on the line of the Antonine Wall, 1 km east of the fort-site at Westerwood, 1868.

Loc.: Hunterian Museum, University of Glasgow. Inv. no. F.16.

Glasgow Herald 15 June 1868; C. Maclagan, *PSAS* ix, 1870–2, pp. 178–9 with fig.; J. Buchanan, ibid., pp. 472–81 with fig.; Macdonald 1897, p. 76, no. 32, pl. xvi; A. Gibb, *Scottish Antiquary* xvi, 1902, pp. 24–7; Macdonald 1934, p. 392; Keppie 1979, p. 20, no. 19; id., *Britannia* xiii, 1982, p. 100.

The left-hand side of the slab is preserved in two adjoining fragments. No part of an inscription remains. The outer mouldings are badly chipped, but the sculptured figures are well preserved.

H.: 0.845 m.; W.: 0.36 m.; D.: 0.145 m.

Relief carving. Local yellow sandstone.

A triangular cramp-hole is set into the left face of the slab.

The slab is bordered by a triple-beaded moulding. The die, which may have been in the shape of a diamond or a hexagon, was enclosed by cable-patterns. In the top left corner, a horned and bearded triton, with twisted tail, holds an anchor reversed in the crook of his right arm. Below, a captive, bound and naked, rests on one knee with his head inclined to the right. The top and bottom right corners of the slab, when complete, would also have contained sculptured figures.

The dimensions of the slab, its findspot on the line of the Antonine Wall away from a fort-site, the figure of a kneeling captive, and (less certainly) the presence of the cramp hole, suggest that it was a distance slab. The die, if diamond or hexagonal in shape, could hardly have contained the usual full-length inscription. It is not possible to establish which legion was responsible. The style has been thought to recall that of slabs of the Second Legion,[1] but the kneeling captive is a common motif, and the style of carving here recalls the captives on no. 149, erected by the Twentieth Legion. Alternatively, from the presence of the triton, the slab may be evidence of the activities of a detachment of the *classis Britannica*, which took part in the building of Hadrian's Wall twenty years before.[2]

    Antonine date (perhaps AD 142–3).

85   Building Stone   PLATE 24

Prov.: Westerwood, Dunbartonshire, at the fort-site, in or before 1725.

Now lost (illustration from Gordon).[3]

Gordon 1726, p. 6, pl. xv.3; Horsley 1732, pp. 200–1, pl. (*Scotland*) xix; Gough 1806, iv, p. 99; Hodgson 1840, p. 265, no. cclxvi; Stuart 1852, p. 343; *CIL* vii, 1102; Macdonald 1934, p. 257; *RIB* 2157.

No measurements given.

Incised. Type of stone not recorded.

On the front face of this stone is the crude representation of an erect *phallus*, with (above) the letters *Nvx*. Below, and separated from the *phallus* by a horizontal line, is an inscription which reads: *ex voto*.

    Antonine date.

---

[1] J. Buchanan, loc. cit.; Macdonald 1897, p. 76; R. W. Feachem, *PSAS* lxxxix, 1955–6, p. 335.   [2] *RIB* 1340.

[3] Horsley's drawing shows the *phallus* concealed by a large fig leaf.

86 Altar to the Silvanae and Quadriviae Caelestes
PLATE 25

Prov.: Turned up by the plough 90 m west of Westerwood fort, 1963.

Loc.: Falkirk Museum.

R. P. Wright, *JRS* liv, 1964, pp. 178–9, no. 1; id., *PSAS* c, 1967–8, pp. 192–3, pl. 23a; *AE* 1964, 175; A. S. Robertson, *The Antonine Wall* 1968, p. 65; L. J. F. Keppie, *GAJ* v, 1976, p. 15.

The back and side faces of the capital, shaft, and base are badly scored by ploughing, and one segment is broken away. The mouldings and edges of the stone have suffered damage. The right-hand bolster is all but lost, and the *focus* is badly chipped. Parts of the die are obscured by a dark, perhaps ferrous, staining.

H.: 0.63 m.; W.: 0.25 m.; D.: 0.27 m.

Letter heights: 1–8: 0.025 m.

Relief carving. Local buff sandstone.

Decoration is confined to the capital. The surviving left-hand bolster terminates in a rosette. The *focus*-mount takes the form of a five-petalled rosette with a raised central boss. On the front face of the capital, between the two bolsters, is a line of three crescentic motifs. The inscription reads: *Silvanis [et] | Quadruis Ca[e]|lestib(us) sacr(um) | Vibia Pacata | Fl(avi) Verecu[nd]i | c(enturio) leg(ionis) VI Vic(tricis) | cum suis | v(otum) s(olvit) l(ibens) m(erito)*.

The dedication is 'to the celestial goddesses of the woodland and the crossroads'. The inscription reveals the presence at Westerwood of the family of a centurion of the Sixth Legion. The man, Flavius Verecundus, may be envisaged as the commander of the fort-garrison. The association of this group of female deities is seemingly unique, and R. P. Wright has argued, from the appearance of the epithet *Caelestibus*, for an African origin for the dedicator, Vibia Pacata; but it must be doubted whether any such localization is possible on the available evidence.

Antonine date.

87 Altar to the Nymphs
PLATE 25

Prov.: Croy Hill, Dunbartonshire, before 1826.

Loc.: National Museum of Antiquities of Scotland, Edinburgh. Inv. no. FV 42.

Gent. Mag. xcvi, 1826, i, p. 166; J. Skinner, *Archaeo-logia* xxi, 1827, p. 467, pl. xxi.2; Stuart 1852, p. 342, pl. xiii.7; *CIL* vii, 1104 with *Addit.* p. 313; *EE* ix, p. 625; Macdonald 1934, p. 423, pl. lxxii.4; *RIB* 2160.

The lower left corner of the altar is a modern restoration. The four bolster-terminals are damaged.

H.: 0.87 m.; W.: 0.41 m.; D.: 0.35 m.

Letter heights: 1–5: 0.045 m.

Relief carving. Local buff sandstone.

On the *focus*-mount is a rosette. The inscription reads: *Nymphis | vexillatio | leg(ionis) VI Vic(tricis) | P(iae) F(idelis) sub Fa/[b]io Libera/[li]*.

Erected to the nymphs by a detachment of the Sixth Legion, otherwise attested at Croy Hill fort.[1]

Antonine date.

88 Dedication to Jupiter Dolichenus
PLATE 25

Prov.: Croy Hill, Dunbartonshire, from the east ditch of the fort, during excavation, 1931.

Loc.: National Museum of Antiquities of Scotland, Edinburgh. Inv. no. FV 47.

R. B. Collingwood and M. V. Taylor, *JRS* xxii, 1932, p. 229; G. Macdonald, *PSAS* lxvi, 1931–2, pp.268–76, figs. 15 and 18; 1934, p. 415, no. 32, pl. xlvii.1; P. Merlat, *Répertoire des inscriptions et monuments figurés du culte de Jupiter Dolichenus* 1951, p. 274, no. 283; Toynbee 1964, p. 168; *RIB* 2158; E. and J. R. Harris, *The Oriental Cults in Roman Britain* 1965, p. 63.

Two fragments of the slab survive: both are chipped and worn. Fragment *a* shows the torso, left arm, and thighs of the god, and fragment *b* the hindquarters and one foreleg of a bovine animal. To the right of the animal is the base and part of the shaft of a pillar. Only the top right-hand corner of the die remains.

a: H.: 0.3 m.; W.: 0.205 m.; D.: 0.185 m. *b*: H.: 0.535 m.; W.: 0.26 m.; D.: 0.2 m.

Letter heights: 1: 0.025–0.04 m.

Relief carving. Local reddish sandstone.

The god is dressed in a short tunic, from the belt of which hang several flaps. A fold of his cloak is looped over the crook of his left arm. A baldric passes diagonally across his chest and supports a sword which hangs behind his back—the pommel is visible beneath his left arm and the scabbard beyond his

---

[1] *RIB* 2161–2.

right hip. One flap of a Phrygian cap can be seen above his left shoulder. The animal on fragment *b* faces left. A human left foot is just visible on its back.

The inscription, which was contained within plain mouldings, reads: *[I(ovi) O(ptimo) M(aximo) Dolic]heno* / [........]*I* / ......

The god may be identified as Jupiter Dolichenus. He is usually portrayed brandishing a double-headed axe in his right hand and a thunderbolt in his left, and standing on the back of a bull which faces right.[1] The animal on fragment *b* lacks the genitals which are usually so prominent in the bulls of Dolichene iconography and is facing in the wrong direction: it is therefore more likely to be the heifer on which the god's consort, Juno Regina, is sometimes depicted.[2] When complete, the relief would have shown Jupiter Dolichenus and his consort standing on the backs of their respective animals within a pillared niche. The bull and heifer may have faced each other across an altar or a tree.[3]

Antonine date.

89   Two Heads

Prov.: Croy Hill, Dunbartonshire, some time in the late eighteenth century.

Now lost.

Stuart 1852, p. 340 n. (a).

In 1826 two heads, one male and one female, apparently 'wrenched violently from the necks of their statues', were seen built into the gable-end of a cottage at Croy. The cottage was demolished before 1852.

No measurements given. Type of stone not recorded.

Antonine date?

90   Gravestone?   PLATE 25

Prov.: Croy Hill, Dunbartonshire, *c.*1802.

Loc.: National Museum of Antiquities of Scotland, Edinburgh. Inv. no. FV 43.

Gent. Mag. xcvi, 1826, i, p. 165; J. Skinner, *Archaeologia* xxi, 1827, pp. 455–8 with pl. xxi; Stuart 1852, pp. 340–2, pl. xiii.4; A. Gibb, *Scottish Antiquary* xvi, 1902, p. 22; G. Macdonald, *PSAS* lvii, 1922–3, pp. 177–80; 1934, p. 446, pl. xlvii.2; Toynbee 1964,

p. 188; K. A. Steer, *Scottish Art Review* x.2, 1965, p. 14; Clarke, Breeze, and Mackay 1980, p. 17.

When found the slab was complete, or almost complete. However, the lower part, said to have borne an inscription, was cut off when the stone was built into a wall at the farmhouse of Nether Croy. The surface of the surviving portion is worn and flaked.

H.: 0.37 m.; W.: 0.36 m.; D.: 0.13 m.

Relief carving. Local buff sandstone.

Three soldiers, bare-headed and with mournful expressions, stand facing the front. Each wears a cuirass with an apron reaching to the knees, and a military cloak, its folds tapering to a single point. The central and left-hand figures rest their left hands upon rectangular shields, and hold weighted javelins upright in their right hands. Their helmets, evidently hanging from straps, are suspended in front of the shields. The figure on the right holds his shield on his left arm at waist height, and his javelin at a slant across his body. His helmet appears to hang from a strap held in his right hand. The central figure is heavily bearded and of a mature age. The others are clean-shaven and youthful.

It is likely that this sculptured fragment formed the upper half of a small grave-slab, perhaps commemorating a father and his two sons. From their equipment it may be concluded that all three were legionaries.[4]

Antonine date.

91   Fragment of Commemorative Slab

PLATE 26

Prov.: Croy Hill, Dunbartonshire, *c.*1802.

Loc.: National Museum of Antiquities of Scotland, Edinburgh. Inv. no. FV 44.

Gent. Mag. xcvi, 1826, i, p. 165; J. Skinner, *Archaeologia* xxi, 1827, p. 458, pl. xxi.1; Stuart 1852, pp. 340–1, pl. xiii.1; *CIL* vii, 1105; A. Gibb, *Scottish Antiquary* xvi, 1902, pp. 21–2; Macdonald 1934, pp. 401–2, no. 20, pl. lxxi.2; Toynbee 1964, p. 148 n. 2; *RIB* 2163.

The left half of the slab is preserved, but the top left corner is broken away. The stone is chipped and worn. The inscription is almost completely lost.

---

[1] See Merlat, op. cit., passim.
[2] See ibid., nos. 153?, 167?, 168.
[3] Cf. ibid. 65, 168, 185, 283, 316; M. P. Speidel, *The Religion of*

Iuppiter Dolichenus in the Roman Army 1978, pls. x, xiv, xxii.
[4] *RIB* 2160–3 (nos. 87, 91) testify to the presence at Croy of a detachment of the Sixth Legion.

H.: 0.58 m.; W.: 0.43 m.; D.: 0.12 m.

Letter heights: 0.045 m.

Relief carving. Local reddish-buff sandstone.

The slab was fashioned to represent a triumphal arch or architectural façade with spiralled columns topped by Corinthian capitals. The inscription was contained within a circular wreath occupying the full width of the central archway, and supported to the left (and presumably also to the right) by winged Cupids crouching on one knee. Within the surviving left-hand niche, a naked Venus advances towards the left, but glances back at a strand of her long hair which she pushes behind her shoulder. From her right hand she trails a robe which passes between her legs. The right-hand niche may have been occupied by a similar figure walking towards the right. Above the side-lintel is part of an unidentifiable motif, perhaps an eagle facing left with its talons resting on the lintel. The inscription reads: [leg(io)] | V[I Vic(trix)] | P[ia F(idelis) f(ecit)].

The slab commemorates work carried out at Croy by the Sixth Legion, otherwise attested at the site.[1]

Antonine date.

92   Altar to Apollo   PLATE 26

Prov.: Auchenvole House, Dunbartonshire, near Bar Hill fort, before 1726.

Loc.: National Museum of Antiquities of Scotland, Edinburgh. Inv. no. FV 14.

Gordon 1726, p. 55, pl. xiii.1–2; Horsley 1732, p. 200, pl. (*Scotland*) xv; Stuart 1852, p. 338, pl. xiii.8; *PSAS* iii, 1857–60, p. 40, no. v; *CIL* vii, 1061; *EE* ix, p. 613; F. J. Haverfield, *Arch. J.* l, 1893, p. 305; Macdonald, 1896, p. 152 n. (i); Macdonald and Park 1906, p. 86; Macdonald 1934, p. 427; *RIB* 2165; Robertson, Scott, and Keppie 1975, p. 31, no. 1; L. J. F. Keppie, *PSAS*, cxiii, 1983, forthcoming.

The altar is badly worn, and the corners of the capital, shaft, and base are broken away. The inscription is almost illegible.

H.: 0.96 m.; W.: 0.43 m.; D.: 0.38 m.

Letter heights: 2–5: 0.045 m.

Relief carving. Local buff sandstone.

Three of the horizontal mouldings on the capital are decorated around all four faces with (from top to bottom) herringbone designs, chevrons, and circular studs. Curving spirals linked the bolsters and *focus*-mount. On the left face of the shaft is a quiver filled with arrows, on the right face is a bow, and on the rear face a large wreath with dependent fillets. The inscription reads: ....*i*|*n*[*i*]   *co*[*h*(*ors*) ..] | *I*........ | *C*[........ | *v*(*otum*)]   *s*(*olvit*)   [*l*(*aeta*) *l*(*ibens*)]   *m*(*erito*). A modern inscription on the rear face of the capital, which incorporates the central roundel below the *focus*-mount, reads: *I*(*ovi*) *O*(*ptimo*) *M*(*aximo*).[2]

The presence of a bow and quiver suggest that the altar was dedicated to Apollo, god of archery. It is possible to restore the inscription to show a dedication by the First Cohort of Hamian archers.

Antonine date.

93   Altar to Mars Camulus   PLATE 27

Prov.: First seen built 'into the wall of a country-house hard by the Roman fort on Bar Hill', c.1733.

Loc.: Hunterian Museum, University of Glasgow. Inv. no. F. 25.

The Daily Gazetteer, 7 Sept. 1736 (as reported by Nichols 1790); Sir John Clerk, letter to R. Gale, 1737, *Surtees Soc.* lxxx (= Stukeley, *Memoirs and Correspondence* iii), 1887, p. 411; Stukeley 1720 (MS note by the author); University of Glasgow 1768, pl. xix; Nichols 1790, pp. 308–9, pl. vi.10; Hodgson 1840, p. 271, no. ccxciv; Stuart 1852, pl. xiii.9; W. T. Watkin, *Arch. J.* xli, 1884, p. 184; *CIL* vii, 1103; *EE* vii, 1093; *EE* ix, p. 624; F. J. Haverfield, *Arch. J.* l, 1893, p. 304, no. 161; Macdonald 1897, p. 69, no. 28, pl. xii; Macdonald and Park 1906, pp. 85–6; Macdonald 1934, p. 426, no. 43, pl. liii.4; *RIB* 2166; Robertson, Scott, and Keppie 1975, p. 32, no. 2; L. J. F. Keppie, *PSAS* cxiii, 1983, forthcoming.

The capital and upper part of the shaft survive. The corners are much damaged, and the inscription almost illegible.

H.: 0.49 m.; W.: 0.32 m.; D.: 0.255 m.

Letter heights: 1–5: 0.03 m.

Relief carving. Local buff sandstone.

On the front and rear faces of the capital, curving spirals (all but lost) linked the *focus*-mount to the bolsters, which may have taken the form of rosettes.

---

[1] *RIB* 2160–2.   [2] *RIB* 2332*.

Two of the capital-mouldings are decorated, around three sides of the altar, with a series of raised circular studs and (above) a row of chevrons. On the left side of the shaft is a knife, on the right a handle-less *patera*. The inscription reads: *Deo Mar(ti)* | *Camulo* | *[m]ilites coh(ortis) [I]* | *Hamioru[m]* | *[.]civ[.]sc[...]* | *[.]ivi[..]*.

The altar was dedicated to Mars Camulus by the First Cohort of *Hamii*, a known garrison at Bar Hill.[1] The Celtic war-god Camulus (or Cumulos) is identified with Mars on several inscriptions from Gaul.[2] The distribution of his cult-centres in Britain is further suggested by the place-names Camulodunum (shared by Colchester in Essex and Almondbury in Yorkshire) and Camulosessa (thought to denote a Roman fort in Southern Scotland).[3]

Antonine date.

94 Altar to Silvanus PLATE 27

Prov.: Castlehill, Dunbartonshire, *c*.225 m. northeast of the east gate of Bar Hill fort, 1895. A rectangular stone slab, hollowed to serve as its plinth, was found nearby.

Loc.: Hunterian Museum, University of Glasgow. Inv. no. F. 24.

F. J. Haverfield, in Glasgow Archaeological Society, *The Antonine Wall Report* 1899, pp. 153–4; *EE* ix, 1242; Macdonald and Park 1906, p. 85; Macdonald 1934, p. 425, no. 42, pl. liii.3; *RIB* 2167; Robertson, Scott, and Keppie 1975, p. 32, no. 3.

The front corners of the capital and shaft are broken away. The workmanship is crude and careless; little effort has been made to differentiate capital, shaft, and base.

H.: 0.92 m.; W.: 0.45 m.; D.: 0.265 m.

Letter heights: 1–6: 0.05 m.

Relief carving. Local buff sandstone.

On the right side of the shaft is a roughly worked, raised oblong which was identified by Haverfield as a bow; it could equally well be a knife. The left side of the shaft is plain. The inscription reads: *D]eo Silv[ano* | *C]aristan[ius* | *I]ustianu[s]* | *praef(ectus)* | *[c]oh(ortis) I Ham[ior(um)]* | *v(otum) s(olvit) l(aetus) l(ibens) m(erito)*.

The altar is a dedication to Silvanus by Caristanius Justianus, prefect of the First Cohort of Hamian archers, one-time garrison at Bar Hill. Justianus may be a member of the distinguished Caristanius family from Pisidian Antioch, one of whom had served as a legionary legate in Britain under Agricola.[4]

Antonine date.

95 Altar PLATE 27

Prov.: Bar Hill, Dumbartonshire, before 1825.

Now lost (illustration from Skinner).

J. Skinner, BM MS *Addit.* 33686, f. 51; *EE* ix, 1243; *RIB* 2168.

Two fragments preserved: (*a*) the capital and a small part of the shaft, and (*b*) the lower part of the shaft and the base.

a: H.: *c*.0.4 m.; W.: —; D.: —. *b*: H.: *c*.0.35 m.; W.: —; D.: —.

Relief carving. Type of stone not recorded.

The bolsters on the capital terminated in plain roundels or scrolls; between them, on the *focus*-mount, may have been another roundel, or a rosette. One of the cornice-mouldings was decorated with a double zigzag line, somewhat reminiscent of the chevron motifs on nos. 92 and 93. The inscription read: *Deo* | *II [......*

Antonine date.

96 Uninscribed Altar PLATE 27

Prov.: Bar Hill, Dunbartonshire, *c*.1725. By 1726 it had passed into the possession of Mr James Glen of Linlithgow.

Now lost (illustration from Gordon).

Gordon 1726, p. 55, pl. xiii.3; Horsley 1732, p. 200; Stuart 1852, p. 338, pl. xiii.3; Macdonald and Park 1906, p. 86; Robertson, Scott, and Keppie 1975, p. 36.

No measurements given.

Relief carving. Type of stone not recorded.

On one side of the shaft was a *patera* with a slender handle pointing downwards, and on the other a jug,

---

[1] L. J. F. Keppie, *PSAS* cxiii, loc. cit.
[2] E.g. Espérandieu 6595 = *CIL* xiii, 8701.
[3] I. A. Richmond, *Archaeologia* xciii, 1949, p. 27; A. L. F.

Rivet and C. Smith, *The Place-names of Roman Britain* 1979, pp. 295–6.
[4] See A. R. Birley, *The Fasti of Roman Britain* 1981, p. 234.

below which was a crudely incised rectangle topped by a gable.[1] It is not clear which was the front face of the shaft.

Antonine date?

97 Male Bust

PLATE 28

Prov.: Bar Hill, Dunbartonshire, 'among the ashes of a rudely constructed hearth' in the north-east corner of the fort, during excavation of the fort-site, 1902–5.

Loc.: Hunterian Museum, University of Glasgow. Inv. no. F.1936.4.

Macdonald and Park 1906, pp. 86–8, no. 2; Macdonald 1934, pp. 445–6, pl. lxxvii.6; Toynbee 1964, p. 107; Robertson, Scott, and Keppie 1975, p. 36, no. 12, fig. 9.

The bust is weathered and chipped, but otherwise complete.

H.: 0.35 m.; W.: 0.29 m.; D.: 0.15 m.

Carved in the round. Local buff sandstone.

The bust is of a bearded man who faces the front with his head tilted slightly upwards and to the right. His left arm has been only casually delineated; it appears to hang by his side. His right arm is folded across his chest, the fist tightly clenched except that the middle finger is thrust forward.

This bust, and nos. 98–100 have been regarded as a group, all representing Silenus, the elderly and normally inebriated companion of Bacchus. It is worth noting, however, that this and no. 98 have thick heads of hair, which would make an identification with Silenus less likely.[2] At any rate this bust and its partner probably served as charms to ward off the evil eye, as the protruding finger indicates.[3] The bases of all three complete busts are carefully squared off, suggesting that they once stood on stone plinths.

Antonine date.

98 Male Bust

PLATE 28

Prov.: Bar Hill, Dunbartonshire, 'among the ashes of a rudely constructed hearth' north of the granary, during excavation of the fort-site, 1902–5.

Loc.: Hunterian Museum, University of Glasgow. Inv. no. F.1936.5.

Macdonald and Park 1906, pp. 86–8, no. 4; Macdonald 1934, pp. 445–6, pl. lxxvii.6; Toynbee 1964, p. 107; Robertson, Scott, and Keppie 1975, p. 38, no. 13, fig. 10.

The bust is fractured across the neck, and the bottom left-hand corner is broken away. The stone is otherwise chipped and worn.

H.: 0.33 m.; W.: 0.275 m.; D.: 0.12 m.

Carved in the round. Local buff sandstone.

The bust is of a bearded man, facing the front with his head angled towards the right. His face, with its round cheeks and fleshy nose, closely resembles the worn features of no. 100. His arms are folded across his chest; both fists are tightly clenched except that the middle finger of each is thrust forward, a gesture designed to ward off the evil eye.[4]

The bust must have stood upon a plinth.

Antonine date.

99 Male Bust

PLATE 28

Prov.: Bar Hill, Dunbartonshire, 'among the ashes of a rudely constructed hearth', in the south-east corner of the fort, during excavation of the fort-site, 1902–5.

Loc.: Hunterian Museum, University of Glasgow. Inv. no. F.1936.3.

Macdonald and Park 1906, pp. 86–8, no. 1; Macdonald 1934, p. 445, pl. lxxvii.6; Toynbee 1964, p. 107; Robertson, Scott, and Keppie 1975, p. 36, no. 11, fig. 9.

The front of the face is lost, and the bottom right corner of the bust is broken away.

H.: 0.27 m.; W.: 0.295 m.; D.: 0.135 m.

Carved in the round. Local buff sandstone.

The bust is of a man, with a bald head and possibly a beard, facing the front and raising a drinking cup or tankard towards his lips.

The angle of his hands suggests that he is grasping the wide handles of a *scyphus* which he appears to be steadying with his palms. The bust would probably have been set upon a plinth. In all probability it represents Silenus (see no. 97).

Antonine date.

---

[1] Stuart 1852, loc. cit. incorrectly shows the *patera* and jug on adjacent sides of the shaft.

[2] Toynbee 1964, loc. cit., suggests that local native deities are represented here.

[3] Cf. Persius, *Sat.* ii. 33; Juv. *Sat.* x. 53; with J. E. B. Mayor, *Thirteen Satires of Juvenal* 1878, ad loc.; C. Sittl, *Die Gebärden der Griechen und Römer* 1890, pp. 101, 123.

[4] Cf. no. 97.

100 Male Head   PLATE 28

Prov.: Bar Hill, Dunbartonshire, 'among the ashes of a rudely constructed hearth' north of the granary, during excavation of the fort-site, 1902–5.

Loc.: Hunterian Museum, University of Glasgow. Inv. no. F.1936.6.

Macdonald and Park 1906, pp. 86–8, no. 3; Macdonald 1934, p. 445, pl. lxxvii.6; Toynbee 1964, p. 107; Robertson, Scott, and Keppie 1975, p. 38, no. 14, fig. 10.

The head has been broken off immediately below the chin. The features are much weathered, the nose being almost totally lost.

H.: 0.12 m.; W.: 0.095 m.; D.: 0.1 m.

Carved in the round. Local buff sandstone.

The head is of a bald-headed, bearded man.

In all probability it formed the upper part of a bust similar to no. 99, and may also represent Silenus.

Antonine date.

101 Tombstone of C. Julius Marcellinus
PLATE 28

Prov.: Seen *c*.1588 built into Kilsyth Castle, Stirlingshire. The reference to the First Cohort of *Hamii* indicates that the tombstone derived from a cemetery at Bar Hill fort, 3 km to the south-west.

Now lost (illustration from Anonymus Germanus).

J. Gruter, Leyden University, MS *Papenbroekianus* 6, f. 110; Anonymus Germanus, BM MS *Cotton Julius* F VI, f. 323; W. Camden, ibid. f. 295; id., *Britannia*, ed. 6, 1607, p. 699 with fig.; Sibbald 1707, p. 49; James Douglas, Earl of Morton, *Ancient Inscriptions on Stones found in Scotland*, before 1786 (MS in Library of Society of Antiquaries, Edinburgh; not now traceable), p. 5; Hodgson 1840, p. 265, no. cclxviii; Stuart 1852, p. 338; *CIL* vii, 1110; *EE* ix, p. 625; Macdonald and Park 1906, p. 85; Macdonald 1934, p. 436, no. 56; *RIB* 2172; L. J. F. Keppie, *GAJ* v, 1978, pp. 22–3.

The upper half of the tombstone survived; it is not clear whether any part of the inscription was lost.

No measurements given. (The slab was described by Camden as 'almost oval and 6 foot in length', but the drawing in *Cotton Julius* does not support such a description.)

Relief carving. Type of stone not recorded.

Above the die was a triangular gable containing a pine-cone and bordered by uncertain motifs, perhaps intended as dolphins. The top corners were decorated with small rosettes. The inscription read: *D(is)* *M(anibus)* / *C(ai) Iuli* / *Marcellini* / *praef(ecti)* / *coh(ortis) I Hamior(um)*.

The inscription identified the deceased as C. Julius Marcellinus, prefect of the First Cohort of *Hamii*, which we know to have formed the garrison at Bar Hill.

Antonine date.

102 Commemorative Slab of Cohors I Baetasiorum   PLATE 28

Prov.: Bar Hill, Dunbartonshire, in the well of the headquarters building, during excavation of the fort-site, 1902.

Loc.: Hunterian Museum, University of Glasgow. Inv. no. F.1936.1.

F. J. Haverfield, *Westdeutsche Zeitschrift, Korrespondenzblatt* xxii, 1903, col. 203, no. 5; id., *Athenaeum*, 6 Feb. 1904, p. 185; id., *EE* ix, 1245; Macdonald and Park, 1906, p. 82, fig. 29; Macdonald 1934, p. 414, no. 31; E. B. Birley, *PSAS* lxxii, 1937–8, p. 283; G. Macdonald, *PSAS* lxxiii, 1938–9, p. 258; *RIB* 2170; Robertson, Scott, and Keppie 1975, 35, no. 9.

The slab is only partially preserved, in three fragments, here designated *a*–*c*. Part of the left-hand edge of the slab is preserved in *a*, and all of the right hand edge in *b* and *c* which adjoin.

a: H.: 0.515 m.; W.: 0.22 m.; D.: 0.14 m. *b* and *c*: H.: 0.605 m.; W.: 0.43 m.; D.: 0.14 m. When complete the slab must have measured *c*.0.96 m. in length.

Letter heights: 1–5: 0.065 m.

Relief carving. Local buff sandstone.

The die is flanked to left and right by columns, with plain capitals and bases. Above, a triple-ridged border serves as an architrave. The inscription reads: *I[mp(eratori) Cae]sari* / *T(ito) Ae[l(io) Had(riano)* *An]tonino* / *Au[g(usto) Pio p(atri) p(atriae) c]oh(ors)* / *I [Baetasior(um) C(ivium)] R(omanorum) ob* / *vi[rtutem et fi]dem*.

Despite the fragmentary condition of the slab, it can be restored with some confidence to record

construction work at Bar Hill by the First Cohort of
Baetasii, otherwise attested in garrison there.

Antonine date.

103 Column Capital PLATE 29

Prov.: Bar Hill, Dunbartonshire, from the well in the
headquarters building, during excavation of the fort-
site, 1902.

Loc.: Hunterian Museum, University of Glasgow.
Inv. no. F.1936.9.

T. Ross, in Macdonald and Park 1906, p. 136, fig. 47;
Macdonald 1934, p. 279, fig. 38; W. Schleiermacher,
Germania xxxviii, 1960, pp. 377–8; Robertson, Scott,
and Keppie 1975, p. 40, no. 22, fig. 11.

The capital is slightly worn but otherwise un-
damaged.

H.: 0.445 m. *Abacus*: H.: 0.125 m.; W.: 0.325 m.; D.:
0.32 m.

Relief carving. Local buff gritstone.

The capital, *torus*, and part of the shaft have been
carved from a single block of stone. The *abacus* is
divided into two bands by a horizontal incised line;
the lower band (0.045 m. high) is decorated with
chevrons.[1] Though the *abacus* is almost exactly
square, there are five complete chevrons on two of the
opposing faces, six on the others; the corners of the
echinus are squared off. The capital is not set directly
above the column but slightly to one side.

This capital, together with nos. 104 and 105, and
many undecorated capitals, shafts (including nos. 106
and 107), and bases, recovered from the well, probably formed a colonnade in the courtyard of the
headquarters building, or a porch along its main
frontage facing the *via principalis*.

Antonine date.

104 Column Capital PLATE 29

Prov.: Bar Hill, Dunbartonshire, from the well in the
headquarters building, during excavation of the fort-
site, 1902.

Loc.: Hunterian Museum, University of Glasgow.
Inv. no. F.1936.8.

T. Ross, in Macdonald and Park 1906, p. 136, fig. 48;

Macdonald 1934, p. 279, fig. 38; Robertson, Scott,
and Keppie 1975, p. 40, no. 21, fig. 11.

The upper part of the capital is chipped and worn.

H.: 0.37 m. *Abacus*: H.: 0.15 m.; W.: 0.3 m.; D.:
0.27 m.

Relief carving. Local buff gritstone.

The *abacus* is divided by a horizontal incised line into
two bands; the lower (0.055 m. high) is decorated
around all four faces with chevrons. On each of
the longer faces of the rectangular *abacus* are four
chevrons, on the shorter faces, three. The angles of
the *echinus* have been roughly squared off.

Antonine date.

105 Column Capital PLATE 29

Prov.: Bar Hill, Dunbartonshire, from the well in the
headquarters building, during excavation of the fort-
site, 1902.

Loc.: Hunterian Museum, University of Glasgow.
Inv. no. F.1936.7.

T. Ross, in Macdonald and Park 1906, pp. 135–6,
fig. 46; Macdonald 1934, p. 444, pl. li. 3; Robertson,
Scott, and Keppie 1975, p. 40, no. 20, fig. 11.

The capital is slightly worn, and the shaft and *torus*
are chipped and cracked.

H.: 0.59 m. (incl. shaft); W.: 0.35 m.; D.: 0.37 m.

Relief carving. Local buff sandstone.

The capital, circular *torus*, and part of the shaft have
been carved from a single block. The bell-shaped
echinus is ornamented around three sides with tall,
upright leaves, roughly carved; there are three complete leaves on each decorated face.

Antonine date.

106 Column Fragment with Corbel PLATE 29

Prov.: Bar Hill, Dunbartonshire, from the well in the
headquarters building, during excavation of the fort-
site, 1902.

Loc.: Hunterian Museum, University of Glasgow.
Inv. no. F.1936.27.

T. Ross, in Macdonald and Park 1906, pp. 138–9 with
fig. 52; Macdonald 1934, p. 444; Robertson, Scott,
and Keppie 1975, p. 38, no. 17, fig. 10.

[1] Schleiermacher, *Germania* xxxviii, 1960, pp. 377–8, compares decorative features on the Bar Hill capitals with a more recent find
from Neckarburken on the Upper German *limes*.

Only a small part of the shaft above and below the corbel is preserved; above, the break occurs across the mortise-pocket. On the left side of the shaft, level with the *bucranium*, is a small squarish hole, 50 mm. across and 50 mm. deep.

Shaft: H.: 0.85 m.; Diam.: 0.32 m. Corbel: H.: 0.295 m.; W.: 0.23 m.; D.: 0.09 m.

Corbel carved in high relief. Local buff sandstone.

The corbel takes the form of a stylized bull's head (*bucranium*) with raised forehead and wide nostrils. The corbel (and no. 107) may have supported a horizontal timber beam, perhaps over a door leading into the headquarters building.

Antonine date.

107   Column Fragment with Corbel   PLATE 29

Prov.: Bar Hill, Dunbartonshire, from the well in the headquarters building, during excavation of the fort-site, 1902.

Loc.: Hunterian Museum, University of Glasgow. Inv. no. F.1936.28.

T. Ross, in Macdonald and Park 1906, pp. 138–9, fig. 52; Macdonald 1934, p. 444; Robertson, Scott, and Keppie 1975, p. 38, no. 17, fig. 10.

The column-shaft has been broken off across the top of the *bucranium*; no trace of a mortise-pocket survives.

Shaft: H.: 1.05 m.; Diam.: 0.33 m. Corbel: H.: 0.29 m.; W.: 0.215 m.; D.: 0.085 m.

Corbel carved in high relief. Local buff sandstone.

The corbel takes the form of a stylized bull's head (*bucranium*), as on no. 106, with which it forms a pair.

Antonine date.

108   Tombstone of Flavius Lucianus   PLATE 29

Prov.: Shirva, Dunbartonshire, in the hollow of the Antonine ditch, re-used in a souterrain, 1729.

Loc.: Hunterian Museum, University of Glasgow. Inv. no. F.36.

Gordon 1732, pp. 6–8, pl. lxvi, fig. vi; Horsley 1732, p. 339, pl. (*Scotland*) xxxiii; University of Glasgow 1768, pl. xviii; Gough 1806, iv, p. 100, pl. lv.3; Hodgson 1840, p. 265, no. cclxvii; Stuart 1852, p. 334, pl. xii.6; *CIL* vii, 1118; Macdonald 1897, pp.

65–6, no. 25, pl. xiv.3; Macdonald 1934, p. 437, no. 57, pl. lxxvi.1; *RIB* 2181.

The tombstone is broken horizontally across the die, and the lower portion is lost. The surviving half is much worn and damaged, especially on the right-hand side.

H.: 0.685 m.; W.: 0.475 m.; D.: 0.215 m.

Letter heights: 1–4: 0.04 m.

Relief carving. Local buff gritstone.

Above the die is a gable containing a rosette against a background of stylized leaves; two smaller rosettes occupy the top corners. The inscription reads: *D(is) M(anibus)* | *Fla(vius) Lucia*/*nus miles* | *leg(ionis) II Aug(ustae)*.

This stone commemorates Flavius Lucianus, a soldier in the Second Legion, who died whilst on service in Scotland. It and nos. 109–14 were found near Shirva, a farmhouse on the line of the Antonine Wall about half-way between the fort-sites at Bar Hill and Auchendavy, during a search for building materials for a field wall in 1728–9. They formed part of a stone-built structure in the hollow of the Antonine ditch, evidently a souterrain of the later Iron Age, presumably constructed by local tribesmen some time after the Roman withdrawal;[1] Alexander Gordon provides a useful sketch.[2] With one exception (no. 114) the stones are funerary, and must derive from a nearby fort cemetery, at Bar Hill or Auchendavy, more probably the latter, where the Second Legion is otherwise attested.[3]

Antonine date.

109   Tombstone of Salmanes   PLATE 30

Prov.: Shirva, Dunbartonshire, in or just north of the hollow of the Antonine Ditch, c.1728.

Loc.: Hunterian Museum, University of Glasgow. Inv. no. F.37.

Gordon 1732, pp. 6–8, pl. lxvi.2; Horsley 1732, p. 199, pl. (*Scotland*) xiii; University of Glasgow 1768, pl. xii; Gough 1806, iv, p. 99, pl. iv.10; Hodgson 1840, p. 266, no. cclxxi; Stuart 1852, pp. 334–5, pl. xii.8; *CIL* vii, 1119; Macdonald 1897, pp. 66–7, no. 26, pl. xv.3; Macdonald 1934, pp. 438–9, no. 59, pl. lxxvi.2; *RIB* 2182.

The slab is fractured horizontally across the die and the edges are damaged in the vicinity of the break.

---

[1] I. A. Richmond and K. A. Steer, *PSAS* xc, 1956–7, p. 5.   [2] Gordon, 1732, pl. lxviA.   [3] See below, nos. 115–16, and *RIB* 2174–9.

The stone is very worn, and the workmanship careless.

H.: 1.215 m.; W.: 0.49 m.; D.: 0.11 m.

Letter heights: 1–2: 0.055 m.; 3: 0.05 m.; 4–5: 0.045 m.

Relief carving. Local buff gritstone.

The die is enclosed within a single incised line, flanked by vertical bands of cable-patterns. Centrally placed above is a garland with dependent fillets; to either side are an incised palm branch and a simple rosette. A crude attempt has been made to give the shape of a gable to the top of the stone. The inscription reads: *D(is) M(anibus)* | *Salmanes* | *vix(it) an(nos)* *XV* | *Salmanes* | *posuit.*

The dedicator, Salmanes, is generally thought to have been a trader from one of Rome's eastern provinces, carrying on his business at or outside an Antonine Wall fort.[1]

Antonine date.

110   Tombstone of Verecunda   PLATE 30

Prov.: Shirva, Dunbartonshire, in the hollow of the Antonine ditch, *c.*1728.

Loc.: Hunterian Museum, University of Glasgow. Inv. no. F.38.

Gordon 1732, pp. 6–8, pl. lxvi.3; Horsley 1732, pp. 199–200, pl. (*Scotland*) xiv; University of Glasgow 1768, pl. xiii; Gough 1806, iv, p. 99, pl. iv.1; Stuart 1852, p. 334, pl. xii.7; *CIL* vii, 1120; Macdonald 1897, pp. 67–8, no. 27, pl. xv.4; Macdonald 1934, p. 439, no. 60, pl. lxxvi.3; *RIB* 2183.

The upper half of the tombstone is preserved in two adjoining fragments (here *a* and *b*). A separate fragment (*c*—unpublished) preserves the lower left corner. Traces of the original red paint are visible in the hollows of the letters.

a and *b*: H.: 0.915 m.; W.: 0.54 m.; D.: 0.15 m. *c*: H.: 0.19 m.; W.: 0.23 m.; D.: 0.13 m.

Letter heights: 1–3: 0.07 m.

Relief carving. Local buff gritstone.

The die is enclosed within a triple plain moulding, and topped by a gable similarly framed. Within the gable is a wreath; single rosettes occupy the top left and top right corners. On *c*, just within the outer

mouldings, is a sculptured motif, perhaps a fish-tail. The inscription reads: *D(is) M(anibus)* | *Verec* | *undae.*

The slab is similar in style and execution to no. 108. The single name, Verecunda, indicates that the deceased was not a Roman citizen.

Antonine date.

111   Tombstone of a Soldier   PLATE 30

Prov.: Shirva, Dunbartonshire, in the hollow of the Antonine ditch, re-used in a souterrain, 1729.

Loc.: Hunterian Museum, University of Glasgow. Inv. no. F.41.

Gordon 1732, pp. 6–8, pls. lxvi.4, lxix.1; Horsley 1732, pp. 198–9, 308, pl. xi; pp. 339–40, pl. (*Scotland*) xxxiii; University of Glasgow 1768, pl. x; Gough 1806, iv, p. 99, pl. iii.9; Laskey 1813, p. 77, no. 10; Hodgson 1840, p. 265; Stuart 1852, p. 334, pl. xii.5; Macdonald 1897, pp. 89–90, no. 39, pl. xiv.2; Macdonald 1934, p. 448, pl. lxxvi.4.

The slab is much weathered and broken off just below the knees of the figure. It presumably formed the upper half of a gravestone. The missing portion may have borne an appropriate inscription.

H.: 0.69 m.; W.: 0.55 m.; D.: 0.14 m.

Relief carving. Local buff gritstone.

A male figure, heavily bearded, stands facing the front, holding a spear upright in his right hand and a handled box in his left. He wears a tunic and over this a military cloak terminating in a double pendant.

The soldier was presumably a member of the garrison at Auchendavy or Bar Hill. The handled box is of the type carried by standard-bearers and clerks serving on the headquarters staff of a unit.[2]

Antonine date.

112   Sepulchral Relief   PLATE 30

Prov.: Shirva, Dunbartonshire, in the hollow of the Antonine ditch, re-used in a souterrain, 1729.[3]

Loc.: Hunterian Museum, University of Glasgow. Inv. no. F.39.

Gordon 1732, pp. 6–8, pl. lxix.2; Horsley 1732, p. 399, pl. (*Scotland*) xxxiii; University of Glasgow

---

[1] A. R. Birley, *The People of Roman Britain* 1979, p. 128, suggests a link with the Hamian archers at Bar Hill.

[2] Cf. E. Hübner, *Arch. Zeitung*, N.S. i, 1868, pp. 40–2 with taf. 5.1; *RIB* 673 (York), 492 (Chester); no. 135 below. But the

box occurs on the tombstones of civilians also, cf. Espérandieu 2826–7.

[3] Gordon, op. cit., pl. lxviA shows the slab *in situ* in the souterrain.

1768, pl. xvii; Gough 1806, iv, p. 100, pl. iv.5; Laskey 1813, p. 77, no. 17; Hodgson 1840, p. 265; Stuart 1852, pp. 333-4, pl. xii.2; Macdonald 1897, pp. 86-8, no. 38, pl. ix.1; F. J. Haverfield, *Arch. J.* lvi, 1899, p. 328; Macdonald 1934, p. 447, pl. lv.2; Toynbee 1964, p. 195.

The raised outer border of the slab is broken away in many places, especially at the top and bottom left corners. The face of the reclining figure is badly worn, as are the hands and some of the folds of his *toga.* The left leg of the couch is lost.

H.: 0.68 m.; W.: 0.98 m.; D.: 0.29 m.

Relief carving. Local buff sandstone.

A bearded male figure, facing the front, reclines upon a couch. He wears a tunic and over this a *toga* reaching to his ankles. His left arm rests on a pillow, and his right arm on his thigh. The lower half of his body is twisted so that his legs, feet, and the end-board of the couch are seen from above. As is usual in scenes of this type, the lower half of the body is rather too short in proportion to the upper part, prominence being given to the head and shoulders of the deceased. Above the legs, a small animal, almost certainly a dog, its head upright and its curled tail erect, faces right, its paws standing on what seems to be a cushion.

The scene is clearly a 'funeral banquet', with the deceased imagined as participating in the feast held by his family and friends to mark the end of their period of mourning. Frequently, but not here, a small table piled with food is placed centrally in front of the couch and the deceased usually holds a wreath, napkin, scroll, goblet, or bunch of grapes. Examples of the scene in Britain are largely confined to the northern frontier, and to the legionary fortresses.[1] The dog, a chthonic symbol in Romano-Celtic iconography, represents faithfulness in Roman art.[2] This relief, and no. 113, seem to form a pair, and may show a man and his wife. They presumably formed part of a larger monument.

Antonine date.

113   Sepulchral Relief   PLATE 30

Prov.: Shirva, Dunbartonshire, in the hollow of the Antonine Ditch, re-used in a souterrain, 1729.

Loc.: Hunterian Museum, University of Glasgow. Inv. no. F.40.

Gordon 1732, pp. 6-8, pl. lxix.2; Horsley 1732, p. 339, pl. (*Scotland*) xxxiii; University of Glasgow 1768, pl. xvi; Gough 1806, iv, p. 100, pl. iv.4; Laskey 1813, p. 77, no. 16; Hodgson 1840, p. 265; Stuart 1852, pp. 333-4, pl. xii.3; F. J. Haverfield, *Arch. J.* lvi, 1899, p. 328; Macdonald 1897, pp. 86-9, no. 37, pl. ix.1; Macdonald 1934, pp. 447-8, pl. lv.1; Toynbee 1964, p. 195.

The slab has a diagonal fracture, and is much worn and chipped. Parts of the outer canopy and the face and left hand of the figure are broken away.

H.: 0.65 m.; W.: 1.015 m.; D.: 0.26 m.

Relief carving. Local buff sandstone.

Within a canopied carriage drawn by two yoked mules, a female figure, clad in a long gown, reclines on her left elbow. In her right hand she holds a napkin or wreath. The lower half of her body is twisted so that the legs, feet, and an end-board or bolster are seen from above. Below, close to the right-hand side of the canopy, is a six-spoked wheel.

Earlier commentators, overlooking the wheel and the yoked animals, interpreted the scene as showing a male reclining at a funeral banquet (as on no. 112). But the carriage is undoubtedly the two-wheeled *carpentum,* in which ladies are shown after death being transported to the next world. A number of parallels from Etruscan and Roman contexts can be adduced.[3] The sculptor here was clearly unfamiliar with, and ill-equipped to deal with, a subject of this sophistication.

Antonine date.

114   Commemorative Slab   PLATE 31

Prov. Shirva, Dunbartonshire, *c.*1728.

Loc.: Hunterian Museum, University of Glasgow. Inv. no. F.18.

Gordon 1732, pp. 5-8, pl. lxvi.1; Horsley 1732, p. 199, pl. (*Scotland*) xii; University of Glasgow 1768, pl. xii; Gough 1806, iv, p. 99, pl. iii.8; Hodgson 1840, p. 265, no. cclxix; Stuart 1852, p. 336, pl. xii.1; *CIL* vii, 1117; Macdonald 1897, p. 64, no. 24,

---

[1] Haverfield, loc. cit.
[2] F. Jenkins, *Latomus* xvi, 1957, pp. 60-76; J. M. C. Toynbee, *Animals in Roman Life and Art* 1973, p. 111.

[3] J. Heurgon, *Daily Life of the Etruscans* 1964, pp. 132-4; C. Daremberg and E. Saglio, *Dictionnaire des Antiquités* I.iii, 1887, s.v. *carpentum.*

pl. x.1; Macdonald 1934, pp. 403–4, no. 24, pl. lxxiii.2; *RIB* 2180.

The left side-panel and the lower left-hand corner of the slab are lost; the fragment shown there on many photographs is modern. The surviving portion is broken into four adjoining parts. The neat dressing of the left edge of the slab suggests that a separate block of stone may have been used for the expected left-hand *pelta*-panel (cf. no. 127).

H.: 0.685 m.; W.: 1.205 m.; D.: 0.18 m.

Letter heights: 1–3: 0.075 m.

Relief carving. Local buff sandstone.

The rectangular die is framed by a double border; the inner consists of acanthus-leaf designs, and the outer of cable-patterns. The horns of the surviving *pelta* terminate in crested bird-heads and the central projection in a plain boss decorated with concentric circles. The inscription reads: *vex(illatio)* | *leg(ionis)* *II* | *[Au]g(ustae)*.

The slab commemorates building work carried out by the Second Legion. The elaborate border closely resembles the ornamentation on two slabs erected by the legion at Corbridge in AD 139–40 (*RIB* 1147–8 = Phillips 1977, 84–5), and on no. 68, the distance slab from Bridgeness.

Antonine date.

115 Altar to Diana and Apollo PLATE 31

Prov.: Auchendavy, Dunbartonshire, in a pit south-west of the fort-site, 1771; together with no. 119, *RIB* 2175–8, and two large iron mallets.

Loc.: Hunterian Museum, University of Glasgow. Inv. no. F.28.

University of Glasgow 1768 (*Suppl. c.* 1771), pl. xxiv; Roy 1793, App. 4 by J. Anderson (dated 1773), pp. 201–4, pl. xxxviii; R. Gough, *Archaeologia* iii, 1786, pp. 118–24, pl. viii; Hodgson 1840, p. 266, no. cclxxiii; Stuart 1852, p. 331, pl. xi.2; *CIL* vii, 1112; *ILS* 4831a; Macdonald 1897, p. 58, no. 19, pl. viii.1; Macdonald 1934, p. 429, no. 46, pl. liv.3; *RIB* 2174.

The altar is fractured diagonally across the shaft; the corners of the capital, base, and shaft are slightly damaged.

H.0.725 m.; W.: 0.31 m.; D.: 0.225 m.

Letter heights: 1–5: 0.035 m.

Relief carving. Local buff sandstone.

The bolsters on the face of the capital terminate in roundels with plain bosses; between them is a rosette. The capital mouldings are bordered by horizontal bands of cable-patterns which run around three sides of the altar. The mouldings on the base are plain, except for one band of cable-patterns extending around all four sides. The inscription reads: *Dianae* | *Apollini* | *M(arcus) Cocc[ei(us)]* | *Firmus* | *c(enturio)* *leg(ionis) II Aug(ustae)*.

This altar, to Diana and Apollo, was one of five found in a pit together with the torso (no. 119 below) and two iron mallets.[1] At least four of the altars (and probably also the fifth, but the inscription is incomplete) were erected by the centurion M. Cocceius Firmus, probably the one-time commander of the Auchendavy garrison.[2]

Antonine date.

116 Dedication to Mars and Victory? PLATE 31

Prov.: Auchendavy, Dunbartonshire, in the yard of the farm overlying the fort-site, 1825.

Now lost (illustration from Skinner).

Gent. Mag. xcvi, 1826, i, p. 166; J. Skinner, *Archaeologia* xxi, 1827, pp. 459–60 with pl. xxi.3; Stuart 1852, p. 332 with pl. xi.5; C. F. Herman, *Göttingische gelehrte Anzeigen* 1846, col. 1416; J. Becker, *BJ* xix, 1853, pp. 106–7; *CIL* vii, 1116; Macdonald 1934, pp. 437–8, no. 58, fig. 53; *RIB* 2179; R. W. Davies, *GAJ* iv, 1976, pp. 103–7.

The fragment formed part of a sculptured slab on which the die was enclosed within a laurel wreath.

No measurements given.

Relief carving. Type of stone not recorded.

Skinner's drawing suggests that the slab was originally circular, but the surviving portion may have flaked away from a larger slab, on which the wreath was supported by flanking figures. The inscription read: *NO......* | *MART MAL.....* | *Victo. mil(es)*

---

[1] The other altars (*RIB* 2175–8) lack ornamentation, and so are excluded from this survey.

[2] On the career of Firmus, see E. B. Birley, *Roman Britain and the Roman Army* 1953, pp. 87–103.

le[g(ionis) II] | Aug(ustae) I Alae ex...... | VLERNIS...... | ......

The fragment was believed by Collingwood and Wright[1] to be part of a tombstone commemorating a soldier of the Second Legion, but it is more likely to have been a building record or a dedication to Mars (or perhaps to Mars and Victory jointly) erected by members of the Second Legion. Whatever interpretation is preferred, the fragment provides further evidence for the presence of the Second Legion at Auchendavy.[2]

Antonine date.

117 Altar?

Prov.: Auchendavy, Dunbartonshire, built into a house on or near the fort-site; first seen 1725.

Now lost.

Gordon 1726, p. 54; Stuart 1852, p. 327.

No measurements given.

Relief carving. Type of stone not recorded.

'A small Altar with a Pediment supported by two Pilasters' is reported by Gordon, but the description could equally well apply to a gravestone. Presumably only the front face was visible.

Antonine date?

118 Altar Plinth?

Prov.: Auchendavy, Dunbartonshire, on the fort-site, before 1852.

Now lost.

Stuart 1852, p. 328 n. (b).

No measurements given.

Relief carving. Type of stone not recorded.

'The ornamented socket of an altar may also be seen.'

Antonine date?

119 Statue   PLATE 31

Prov.: Auchendavy, Dunbartonshire, in a pit southwest of the fort-site, 1771, together with no. 115, RIB 2175-8 and two large iron mallets.

Loc.: Hunterian Museum, University of Glasgow. Inv. no. F.45.

University of Glasgow 1768 (Suppl. c.1771), pl. xxxi; Roy 1793, App. 4 by J. Anderson (dated 1773), pp. 201-4, pl. xxxviii; Stuart 1852, p. 295, pl. vii.4; Macdonald 1897, p. 92, no. 42, pl. ii.1; Macdonald 1934, p. 445, pl. lxxvii.2.

It is doubtful whether the statue ever extended below the waist or had arms: the underside is neatly finished off. The surviving torso is badly chipped.

H.: 0.23 m.; W.: 0.235 m.; D.: 0.11 m.

Carved in the round. Local yellowish-buff sandstone.

A series of deeply incised zigzags appears to represent draperies or armour. Around the neck is a cable-pattern which serves to fringe the garment. Above is a series of circular studs, perhaps meant as a necklace or torc.

The figure may have been a local deity. Armless statues occur in Celtic art in Gaul.[3]

Antonine date.

120 Tombstone?

Prov.: Auchendavy, Dunbartonshire, built into an outhouse of the farmstead, before 1852.

Now lost.

Stuart 1852, p. 328 n. (b).

No measurements given.

Relief carving. Type of stone not recorded.

'A small stone with a figure of a Roman soldier rudely sculptured on it' is reported.

Perhaps this was a gravestone similar in scale to no. 90.

Antonine date?

121 Fragment of a Sculptured Slab

Prov.: Auchendavy, Dunbartonshire, dug out of a field on or near the fort-site, before 1852.

Now lost.

Stuart 1852, p. 329 n. (a).

No measurements given.

Relief carving. Type of stone not recorded.

'A fragment of a finely ornamented tablet' is reported to have been found at Auchendavy, and to have passed by 1852 into the collection of Mr John Buchanan.

Antonine date?

---

[1] On RIB 2179.   [2] Cf. RIB 2174-7, 2180-2.   [3] J. V. S. Megaw, Art of the European Iron Age 1970, no. 232.

122 Distance Slab of the Sixth Legion

PLATE 31

Prov.: Near Inchbelly Bridge, Dunbartonshire, c.1740.

Loc.: Hunterian Museum, University of Glasgow. Inv. no. F.2.

Sir John Clerk to R. Gale, letter of 1740, in Nichols 1790, p. 344, with pl. vi.14; T. Routh to R. Gale, letter of 1741, in *Surtees Soc.* lxxx (= Stukeley, *Memoirs and Correspondence* iii), 1887, p. 419; Maitland 1757, p. 178; University of Glasgow 1768, pl. xx; Hodgson 1840, p. 271, no. ccxcv; Stuart 1852, p. 334, pl. x.5; *CIL* vii, 1121; *EE* ix, p. 626; Macdonald 1897, pp. 55–6, no. 18, pl. vii.3; A. Gibb, *Scottish Antiquary* xvi, 1902, pp. 124–6; Macdonald 1934, p. 336, no. 3, pl. lxii.2; *RIB* 2185; Keppie 1979, p. 13, no. 3.

The slab is broken diagonally across the die and the edges and corners are chipped and worn.

H.: 0.77 m.; W.: 1.59 m.; D.: 0.165 m.

Letter heights: 1–4: 0.07 m.; 5–6: 0.06 m.

Relief carving. Local buff gritstone. Two triangular cramp-holes are set into the top face of the slab.

The die is set within a raised moulding, plain to left and right, but triple-ribbed above and below. It is flanked by *peltae* whose horns terminate in griffin-heads, and the central projections in rosettes. Incised six-pointed rosettes embellish the centre of each *pelta*. The inscription reads: *Imp(eratori) Caesari T(ito) | Aelio Hadriano | Antonino Aug(usto) | Pio p(atri) p(atriae) vexilla(tio) | leg(ionis) VI Vic(tricis) P(iae) F(idelis) | per m(ilia) p(assuum).....*

The slab records the completion of a sector of the Antonine Wall, running eastwards from Inchbelly, by the Sixth Legion. The numerals indicating the length of the sector have not been inserted, but there is no need to suppose that the slab is a 'waster'.[1] On the contrary its find-spot on the line of the Wall at a known change-over point between legions VI and XX suggests that it was utilized in its intended position. Sir George Macdonald supposed that the distance recorded was 1000 paces (i.e. *mille passus*),[2] but it is more likely that space was deliberately left for the insertion of the precise distance, when it became known.

Antonine date (probably AD 142–3).

123 Distance Slab of the Twentieth Legion

PLATE 32

Prov.: Eastermains, Dunbartonshire, in the Antonine ditch, 1789.

Loc.: Hunterian Museum, University of Glasgow. Inv. no. F.3

Hodgson 1840, p. 271, no. ccxciii, p. 439; Stuart 1852, p. 325 n. (*a*), pl. x.4; *CIL* vii, 1122; *EE* ix, p. 627; A. Gibb, *Scottish Antiquary* xvi, 1902, pp. 119–21; Macdonald 1934, p. 367, no. 4, pl. lxiii.1; *RIB* 2184; Keppie 1979, p. 13, no. 4.

The outer moulding is chipped and broken away at the bottom left corner. The slab is wedge-shaped, perhaps for insertion into a masonry structure.

H.: 0.44 m.; W.: 0.59 m.; D.: 0.365 m.

Letter heights: 1–2: 0.055 m.; 3: 0.03 m.; 4: 0.035 m.

Relief carving. Local buff sandstone.

A raised ansate panel contains the first two lines of the inscription. Below, a boar emerges from a cave, or from behind a rocky outcrop, and runs right towards a leafy tree. The façade of the outcrop bears the third and fourth lines of the inscription. Two layers of stone blocks serve to roof the outcrop. The inscription reads: *leg(io) XX | V(aleria) V(ictrix) fec(it) | m(ilia) p(assuum) III p(edum) | IIICCCIV.*

The slab records the completion of $3660\frac{4}{5}$ paces of the Antonine Wall, between Eastermains and Bogton, by a detachment of the Twentieth Legion. A tree is sometimes associated with a boar in Celtic iconography,[3] but its significance (if any) for the Twentieth Legion is not known.

Antonine date (probably AD 142–3).

124 Altar?

PLATE 32

Prov.: Kirtintilloch, Dunbartonshire, or near on the fort-site, 'many years' before 1852.

Now lost (illustration from Skinner).

J. Skinner, BM MS *Addit.* 33686, fols. 54–8 with fig.; Stuart 1852, p. 324 n. (*a*); G. Macdonald, *PSAS* lix, 1924–5, p. 293.

No measurements given.

Relief carving. Type of stone not recorded.

'A stone having sculptured on it, in bold relief, the head of a bull with distended nostrils and a fillet

---

[1] Macdonald 1897, p. 56. [2] Macdonald 1934, p. 381; so R. P. Wright, on *RIB* 2185. [3] Ross 1967, pp. 308–10.

across the forehead . . . It appears to have been broken violently off a ponderous mass.'[1] The stone incorporated a panel with an inscription, but by 1852 this was illegible. Skinner supposed the stone to have been the base of an altar.

Antonine date?

125 Fragment of Commemorative Slab

PLATE 32

Prov.: Cadder, Lanarkshire, close to the entrance to the headquarters building, during excavation of the fort-site, 1929–31.

Loc.: Hunterian Museum, University of Glasgow. Inv. no. F.1933.1.

Clarke 1933, pp. 36, 81.

H.: 0.175 m.; W.: 0.15 m.; D.: 0.1 m.

The fragment, which is somewhat worn, preserves a small part of a commemorative tablet, including its lower edge.[2]

Relief carving. Local buff sandstone.

The lower border of the slab was decorated with horizontal bands of leaf-motifs and cable-patterns. Above, is a segment of a wreath, with a fillet to the left.

The find-spot suggests that the fragment belonged to an inscribed slab set above the entrance to the headquarters building. The leafy border invites comparison with nos. 68 and 114, erected by the Second Legion, which is otherwise known to have undertaken construction work at Cadder.[3]

Antonine date.

126 Fragment of Sculptured Slab   PLATE 32

Prov.: Cadder, Lanarkshire, in a pit near the north gateway, during excavation of the fort-site, 1929–31.

Loc.: Hunterian Museum, University of Glasgow. Inv. no. F.1933.2.

Clarke 1933, pp. 43, 81.

The fragment preserves one corner of a sculptured slab.

H.: 0.125 m.; W.: 0.17 m.; D.: 0.06 m.

Relief carving. Local buff sandstone.

Within a plain outer moulding are two S-shaped spirals separated by a bead-and-reel motif.

Antonine date.

127 Distance Slab of the Second Legion

PLATE 32

Prov.: First seen at Cawder House, Lanarkshire, in or shortly before 1588; it may once have stood on the line of the Antonine Wall at nearby Bogton.[4]

Loc.: Hunterian Museum, University of Glasgow. Inv. no. F.4.

J. Gruter, in Leyden University Library, MS *Papenbroekianus* 6, f. 92, 110; J. Scaliger, *Thesaurus Temporum Eusebii Pamphili* 1606, *Animadversiones*, p. 175; W. Camden, BM MS *Cotton Julius* F VI, f. 293; id., *Britannia* 1607, p. 699 with fig.; Sibbald 1697, p. 205; 1707, p. 50; Stukeley 1720, MS gloss in author's hand at p. 10 with fig.; Gordon 1726, p. 50, pl. x.2; Horsley 1732, p. 198, pl. (*Scotland*) x; University of Glasgow 1768, pl. xi; Hodgson 1840, p. 267, no. cclxxvii; Stuart 1852, p. 319, pl. x.2; *CIL* vii, 1126; *EE* ix, pp. 627–8; Macdonald 1897, p. 44, no. 15, pl. vii.2; A. Gibb, *Scottish Antiquary* xvi, 1902, pp. 171–3; Macdonald 1934, p. 369, no. 5, pl. lxiii.2; *RIB* 2186; Keppie 1979, p. 13, no. 5.

The slab is badly weathered and pock-marked; some of the hollows are infilled with mortar. Two small triangular cramp-holes have been set into the top of the slab.

H.: 0.635 m.; W.: 1.005 m.; D.: 0.175 m.

Letter heights: 1–2: 0.08 m.; 3: 0.085 m.; 4: 0.08 m.

Relief carving. Local buff sandstone.

The die is bordered by plain triple mouldings, and flanked to the left by an ansate panel containing a worn six-pointed rosette. At first sight a matching right-hand side-panel seems lost. However, the dressing on the right edge matches the rest, and the cramp-holes are symmetrically placed for the stone as we have it. Perhaps a separate block of stone bore the missing panel. The inscription reads: *Imp(eratori) Caes(ari) Tito Aelio | Hadriano Antonino | Aug(usto)*

---

[1] Stuart 1852, loc. cit.
[2] Clarke, op. cit. p. 36 speaks of two fragments found together, but elsewhere (p. 81) refers only to one. The second fragment could be no. 126, but the two clearly belong to different slabs.

[3] See *RIB* 2188, which is not, so far as can be established, part of the same slab.
[4] Macdonald 1934, p. 371.

Pio p(atri) p(atriae) leg(io) II Aug(usta) | per m(ilia) p(assuum) IIIDCLXVIs.

The slab commemorates the completion of 3666½ paces of the Antonine Wall by the Second Legion, between Summerston and Bogton. The other (western) end of the sector was marked by no. 137.

Antonine date (probably AD 142–3).

128 Commemorative Slab of the Second Legion PLATE 32

Prov.: Unknown, but first seen at Cawder House, Bishopbriggs, to whose owner it was presented by John Napier of Merchiston, between 1572 and 1588.

Loc.: Built into an internal wall at Cawder House, now a Golf Club.

J. Gruter, MS *Papenbroekianus* 6, f. 110; J. Scaliger, *Thesaurus Temporum Eusebii Pamphili* 1606, *Animadversiones*, p. 175; W. Camden, BM MS *Cotton Julius* F VI, f. 295; id., *Britannia* 1607, p. 699 with fig.; Sibbald 1697, p. 205; 1707, pl. at p. 52; Stukeley 1720, p. 8 with fig.; Gordon 1726, p. 54, pl. xii.1; Horsley 1732, p. 198, pl. (*Scotland*) ix; Hodgson 1840, p. 287, no. cclxviii; Stuart 1852, pp. 318–19, pl. x.1; *CIL* vii, 1127; *EE* ix, p. 627; A. Gibb, *Scottish Antiquary* xvi, 1902, pp. 171–3; Macdonald 1934, p. 293, n. 6, pp. 371, 404, no. 26, pl. lxxiii.3; *RIB* 2209.

The stone has suffered damage to its upper margin, and the sculptured reliefs are rather worn.

H.: 0.61 m.; W.: 0.77 m.; D.: —.

Letter heights: 1–3: 0.05 m.; 4: 0.04 m.

Relief carving. Local buff sandstone.

Within triple plain mouldings a laurel wreath, its apex crowned by a rosette, is supported by two Cupids. Below, to left and right, in place of the usual fillets, are mouldings of uncertain significance, perhaps cornucopiae, laid horizontally. Two eagle-heads have sometimes been discerned, rising above, or emerging from behind, the cornucopiae, but the sculptures may have been intended rather to represent the overflowing contents of the horns. The inscription reads: *leg(io) | II | Aug(usta) | fec(it)*.

The slab records construction work by the Second Legion, probably at one of the Antonine Wall forts, but its provenance remains uncertain.

Antonine date.

129 Statue of Mars PLATE 33

Prov.: Balmuildy, Lanarkshire, during excavation of the annexe east of the fort-site, 1914, together with nos. 130–1.

Loc.: Hunterian Museum, University of Glasgow. Inv. no. F.1922.8.

Miller 1922, pp. 56, 61, no. 10, pl. xxix, p. 103; Macdonald 1934, pp. 434–5, no. 54, pl. lxxv.3; *RIB* 2337*; Toynbee 1964, p. 68 n. 4; L. J. F. Keppie, Beverly J. Arnold, and J. K. Ingham, *GAJ* ix, 1982, pp. 73–5.

The right arm and shoulder, the left fore-arm, and the legs between knee and ankle, are lost. The illustration shows the statue as restored in 1979.

H.: 0.8 m.; W.: 0.27 m.; D.: 0.175 m.

Carved in the round. Local buff sandstone.

The god is heavily bearded. He wears a crested helmet, a breastplate with an apron reaching to his knees, and a cloak which is fastened at his right shoulder and hangs down over his left side. At his waist, secured by a belt, is a sword with a large pommel. A faint vertical ridge running down his right thigh may represent a spear shaft. His legs are protected by greaves; the right kneecap is decorated with a Medusa head. On his feet are a pair of plain sandals. Semicircular incisions on the base were read by Miller as the letters CO . . . ., but are more probably decorative.

The statue has been restored to show the god's left hand resting on an oval shield and his right hand clasping a spear close to his shoulder; but the arm may have been raised further, with the spear grasped just below its head.

Antonine date.

130 Altar to Mars PLATE 33

Prov.: Balmuildy, Lanarkshire, during excavation of the annexe east of the fort-site, 1914, together with nos. 129, 131.

Loc.: Hunterian Museum, University of Glasgow. Inv. no. F.1922.5.

F. J. Haverfield, *Roman Britain in 1914* 1915, p. 29, no. 1 with fig.; Miller 1922, pp. 56, 61, no. 9, pl. xxix, p. 103; Macdonald 1934, p. 433, no. 51, pl. lvii.2; *RIB* 2190.

The capital and upper part of the die are preserved in four main fragments.[1] The back of the altar is broken away.

H.: 0.43 m.; W.: 0.36 m.; D.: 0.12 m.

Letter heights: 1–2: 0.035 m.

Relief carving. Local buff sandstone.

Centrally placed on the front face of the capital is a small bust, presumably of Mars, within a semi-circular double-ribbed archway. The god appears to have been helmeted and bearded; he wears a cloak which leaves the right shoulder bare. The inscription reads: *Dio* / [*Ma*]*rti s*[. . . . .

  Antonine date.

131 Statue of Victory   PLATE 33

Prov.: Balmuildy, Lanarkshire, during excavation of the annexe east of the fort-site, 1914, together with nos. 129–30.

Loc.: Hunterian Museum, University of Glasgow. Inv. no. F.1922.9.

Miller 1922, pp. 56, 60–1, nos. 7–8, pl. xviii, p. 103; Macdonald 1934, p. 446, pl. lxxvii.4.

The head and the feet of the statue are lost; the torso is fractured horizontally at the waist, and the edges in the vicinity of the break are much worn.

H.: 0.56 m.; W.: 0.33 m.; D.: 0.1 m.

High relief carving. Local buff sandstone. The workmanship is crude and the folds of the drapery rigidly patterned.

The statue is a representation of Victory. Her wings are visible on the right of the statue and in the crook of her right arm. In her left hand she carries a palm branch; her right hand is raised. Her draperies are so arranged as to leave the right leg bare.

  Comparison with other representations of the goddess suggest that she carried a small wreath in her right hand and that her right foot stood upon a globe.
  Antonine date.

132 Fragment of Statue   PLATE 33

Prov.: Balmuildy, Lanarkshire, during excavation of the fort-site and annexe, 1912–14.

---

[1] An extra fragment, filling the gap in the mouldings at the right side of the capital, is illustrated by Miller and by Macdonald, but cannot now be traced. Further damage was sustained accidentally

Loc.: Hunterian Museum, University of Glasgow. Inv. no. F.1922.11/1.

Unpublished.

The fragment shows the thumb and finger of a right hand resting against or supporting something.

H.: 0.105 m.; W.: 0.045 m.; D.: 0.075 m.

Carved in the round. Local buff sandstone.

It is not clear which way the hand was positioned; if downwards, then it may have held a club or rested upon a shield; if upwards, it may have held a spear. From its proportions, the style of carving and type of sandstone, it might be suspected that the fragment is the missing right hand of the Mars statue described above (no. 130), but repeated attempts at incorporating it into the restoration have proved unsuccessful.

  Antonine date.

133 Female Head   PLATE 33

Prov.: Balmuildy, Lanarkshire, in the cold bath of the annexe bathhouse, 1944.

Loc.: Hunterian Museum, University of Glasgow. Inv. no. F.1922.10.

Miller 1922, p. 60, no. 6, pl. xxvii; Macdonald 1934, p. 446, pl. lxxvii.3.

The lower part of the face is badly damaged.

H.: 0.13 m.; W.: 0.09 m.; D.: 0.095 m.

Carved in the round. Local buff sandstone.

The head is clearly female, her hair rigidly patterned in the Celtic manner. Miller, followed by Macdonald, saw the head as belonging to the torso (no. 134 below) found with it, but the sandstone is of a different texture. Although the separate carving of heads was common Romano-Celtic practice, there is no dowel-hole on the underside of the head to provide a means of attachment, so that it seems to have belonged to a separate statue.

  Antonine date.

134 Torso   PLATE 33

Prov.: Balmuildy, Lanarkshire, in the cold bath of the annexe bathhouse, during excavation, 1914.

---

in 1975, but restoration is in progress. An altar-base from the Balmuildy excavations (F.1922.6) may preserve the lower half of this dedication.

Loc.: Hunterian Museum, University of Glasgow. Inv. no. F.1922.10.

Miller 1922, p. 60, no. 6, pl. xxvii; Macdonald 1934, p. 446, pl. lxxvii.3.

The fragment preserves the upper half of a torso of about one-third life-size. The lower arms are lost, and part of the left shoulder is broken away.

H.: 0.24 m.; W.: 0.29 m.; D.: 0.13 m.

High relief carving. Local buff sandstone.

The figure is clad in a tunic with sleeves to the elbow. From the angle of the upper arms the figure appears to have been carrying some wide object, perhaps a shell, as on no. 151, and may therefore represent a water-nymph.

Antonine date.

135 Commemorative Slab of the Second Legion
PLATE 34

Prov.: Balmuildy, Lanarkshire, in front of the north gateway, during excavation of the fort-site, 1912.

Loc.: Hunterian Museum, University of Glasgow. Inv. no. F.1922.1–3.

EE ix, 1390; F. J. Haverfield, *Roman Britain in 1913* 1914, p. 11, fig. 3; Miller 1922, pp. 57–9, pls. xxv, xxvi; Macdonald 1934, pp. 405–6, no. 28, pl. lvii.1; *RIB* 2192; Toynbee 1964, p. 187; L. J. F. Keppie, *GAJ* iv, 1976, pp. 99–102 with fig.

Five small fragments of the slab (here designated *a–e*) survive. *a*: H.: 0.3 m.; W.: 0.33 m. *b*: H.: 0.495 m.; W.: 0.405 m. *c*: H.: 0.645 m.; W.: 0.24 m. *d*: H.: 0.495 m.; W.: 0.465 m. *e*: H.: 0.475 m.; W.: 0.375 m. In each case, D.: 0.265 m.

Letter heights: 0.01 m.

Relief carving. Local buff sandstone.

Fragment *a* shows the head and foreparts of a capricorn, swimming towards the left; fragments *b*, *c*, and *d* preserve small portions of the inscription; on *d* the die is flanked by a *pelta*. Fragment *e*, which preserves the bottom right corner of the slab, shows a standard-bearer, clad in a tunic and military cloak, facing the front and probably bearded, with the pole of his standard in his left hand and a handled box (cf. no. 111) in his right. Near the base of the pole can be seen a handle to facilitate its removal from the ground. The inscription reads: [*Im*]*p*(*eratori*) *C*(*aesari*)

[*T*(*ito*) *Ael*(*io*) *Hadr*(*iano*) *Anto*/*nin*]*o* [*Aug*(*usto*) *Pio p*(*atri*) *p*(*atriae*) *leg*(*io*)] *II* | [*Aug*(*usta*) *fec*(*it*) *sub* *Q*(*uinto*) *Lo*]*llio* | [*Vrbico leg*(*ato*) *Aug*(*usti*) *pr*(*o*)] *pr*(*aetore*).

Enough survives to indicate that when complete the die was flanked to left and right by *peltae*, whose terminals perhaps took the form of griffin-heads, a favourite device of craftsmen of the Second Legion (cf. nos. 68, 152, 154). In the left-hand side-panel was a capricorn, one of the emblems of the legion, with space above (or below) for a second figure, perhaps a pegasus, its other emblem. In the right-hand panel was a standard-bearer, holding what was probably a *vexillum* bearing the inscription *leg*(*io*) | *II* | *Aug*(*usta*), as on no. 68. To his left there was perhaps another upright figure, possibly a winged Victory as on no. 137. The overall dimensions of the slab can be estimated at 3.5 m. long by 0.76 m. high. It must have been one of the largest erected anywhere on the line of the Antonine Wall. The findspot suggests that the slab was set up over the north gate to commemorate its construction in AD 142–3, during the governorship of Q. Lollius Urbicus.

Antonine date (probably AD 142–3).

136 Sculptured Stones

Prov.: Balmuildy, Lanarkshire, built into cottages on the fort-site; seen in or soon after 1800.

Now lost.

Stuart 1852, p. 320 n. (*a*); Miller 1922, p. 57; L. J. F. Keppie, *GAJ* iv, 1976, pp. 99–102.

'Finely sculptured stones, one in particular with a human figure in high relief and wreaths of flowers.'[1]

Antonine date?

137 Distance Slab of the Second Legion
PLATE 34

Prov.: Summerston Farm, Lanarkshire, on the line of the Antonine Wall, before 1694.

Loc.: Hunterian Museum, University of Glasgow. Inv. no. F.5.

T. Tanner, letter of 1699 to E. Gibson, in J. Nichols (ed.), *Letters on various Subjects . . . to and from William Nicolson* i, 1809, p. 338, no. 6; Sibbald 1707, p. 49; Stukeley 1720, p. 10, fig. 5; Gordon 1726, p. 52,

---

[1] J. Buchanan, in Stuart 1852, loc. cit.

pl. xi.3; Horsley 1732, p. 195, pl. (*Scotland*) iii;
Maitland 1757, p. 181; University of Glasgow 1768,
pl. iii; Laskey 1813, p. 76, no. 3; Hodgson 1840,
p. 268, no. cclxxxv; R. Wodrow, *Analecta* iv, 1843,
p. 66; Stuart 1852, pp. 307-8, pl. ix.1; *CIL* vii, 1130;
EE ix, p. 628; Macdonald 1897, p. 34, no. 10, pl. iii.2;
A. Gibb, *Scottish Antiquary* xvi, 1902, pp. 173-82;
Macdonald 1934, pp. 373-6, no. 6, pl. lxiv.1; *RIB*
2193; Toynbee 1964, p. 149; Keppie 1979, p. 14, no. 6.

The slab is fractured diagonally across the die and
several fragments near the break are lost; the slab is
otherwise rather worn.

H.: 0.6 m.; W.: 1.36 m.; D.: 0.125 m.

Letter heights: 1: 0.075 m.; 2: 0.081 m.; 3: 0.084 m.;
4: 0.08 m.; 5: 0.045 m.

Relief carving. Local buff sandstone.

Two triangular cramp-holes are set into the top of the
slab. Traces of the original red paint were observed
during cleaning in 1979 in the left-hand side-panel
and in the lettering of the inscription.

   The die is enclosed within a plain moulding
and flanked by sculptured scenes. On the left a
winged Victory prepares to crown a cavalryman
who rides down two naked, bearded captives, who
sit with their arms secured behind their backs.
Shields, daggers, and two crossed spears[1] lie on
the ground nearby. The cavalryman, in a crested
helmet and with a short sword hanging from a
baldric, holds an oval shield at shoulder height in
his left hand, and a raised spear, pointing downwards, in his right. His horse, too small in proportion to its rider, prances towards the right, its tail
erect. Victory, with one wing visible over her right
shoulder, stands three-quarters front, and holds
the wreath with both hands. In the right-hand panel,
an eagle, with its head turned towards the left,
appears to perch upon the back of a capricorn, which
swims to the right. Below, another naked and bound
captive, probably clean-shaven, sits with his legs
stretched out to the left. His shield lies close by.
The inscription reads: *Imp(eratori) Caes(ari) Tito
Aelio | Hadriano Antonino | Aug(usto) Pio p(atri)
p(atriae) leg(io) II | Aug(usta) pep m(ilia) p(assuum)
IIIDC|LXVIs.*

   The slab commemorates the construction of 3666½
paces of the Antonine Wall, between Summerston
and Bogton, by a detachment of the Second Legion.

The other (eastern) end of the sector was marked by
no. 127. In design, but not in standard of execution,
the left-hand panel closely resembles that of the
distance slab from Bridgeness (no. 68).
   Antonine date (probably AD 142-3).

138 Distance Slab of the Sixth Legion

PLATE 35

Prov.: East Millichen Farm, Lanarkshire, *c.*100 m.
south of the line of the Antonine Wall, 1803.

Loc.: Art Gallery and Museum, Kelvingrove, Glasgow. Inv. no. '42-18.

J. Reekie, *Glasgow Courier* 5 Mar. 1803; Stuart 1852,
pp. 314-15, pl. xvi.3; *CIL* vii, 1131: *EE* ix, p. 628;
A. Gibb, *Scottish Antiquary* xvii, 1902, p. 27; Macdonald 1934, pp. 376-7, no. 7, pl. lxiv.2; *RIB* 2194;
Keppie 1979, p. 14, no. 7.

The slab is fractured vertically across the die, and
small fragments near the break are lost. The bottom
left and top right corners are broken away, and
the slab is otherwise much chipped and worn by pro-
longed exposure to the elements.

H.: 0.76 m.; W.: 1.45 m.; D.: 0.165 m.

Letter heights: 1: 0.08 m.; 2: 0.07 m.; 3-6: 0.065 m.

Relief carving. Local buff sandstone.

The die is set within a raised moulding, triple-ribbed
above and below, and plain to left and right. It is
flanked by *peltae*, the horns of which terminate in
griffin-heads and the central projections in rosettes.
The inscription reads: *Imp(eratori) Caes(ari) T(ito) |
Aelio Hadri(ano) | Antonino Aug(usto) | Pio p(atri)
p(atriae) vexilla(tio) | leg(ionis) VI Vic(tricis) P(iae)
F(idelis) | per m(ilia) p(assuum) IIIDCLxvis.*

   The slab commemorates the completion of 3666½
paces of the Antonine Wall, between Summerston
and Castlehill, by a detachment of the Sixth Legion.
The other (western) end of the sector was marked by
no. 145.
   Antonine date (probably AD 142-3).

139 Head of a Goddess   PLATE 35

Prov.: Bearsden, Dunbartonshire, during excavation
of the Cold Plunge of the annexe bathhouse, 1973.

Loc.: Hunterian Museum, University of Glasgow.
Inv. no. F.1983.1.

D. J. Breeze, *Current Archaeology* 42, Jan. 1974,
pp. 209-13, with pl.; id., *The Roman Fort at Bearsden,*

---

[1] Earlier commentators identified these motifs as standards, but see J. N. G. Ritchie, *Scottish Archaeological Forum* i, 1969, p. 35.

1973 Excavations 1974, p. 19 with pl.; id., *Archaeological Excavations 1973* (Dept. of the Environment) 1974, p. 110; D. R. Wilson, *Britannia* v, 1974, p. 405; D. J. Breeze, *The Roman Fort at Bearsden* (forthcoming).

The head, presumably from a statue or bust of about half life-size, is only slightly worn, but the nose is broken away. The front of the face was sheared off at the time of discovery, but has been restored.

H.: 0.17 m.; W.: 0.11 m.; D.: 0.15 m.

Carved in the round. Local yellow-buff sandstone.

The head is female, with broad, slightly down-turned lips and full, lentoid eyes. The hair is waved at the front, with a central parting. Rising from the head, towards the back, is a roll of hair or a headdress.[1]

The head is typically Romano-Celtic in style, and perhaps represents a local goddess (cf. above, nos. 20, 133); the findspot has prompted an identification with Fortuna, often venerated in military bathhouses (cf. above, no. 76).

Antonine date.

140 Fountain-head   PLATE 35

Prov.: Bearsden, Dunbartonshire, during excavation of the annexe bathhouse, just south of the changing-room, 1973.

Loc.: Hunterian Museum, University of Glasgow. Inv. no. F.1983.2.

D. J. Breeze, *Current Archaeology* 42, Jan. 1974, pp. 209-13, with pl.; id., *The Roman Fort at Bearsden, 1973 Excavations* 1974, p. 19, pl. 11; id., *Archaeological Excavations 1973* (Dept. of the Environment) 1974, p. 110; id., *The Roman Fort at Bearsden* (forthcoming).

The right hand side of the fountain-head is broken away. Slight damage has been sustained to the nose, mouth, and chin, and there is a crack across the right cheek.

H.: 0.25 m.; W.: 0.26 m.; D.: 0.29 m.

Relief carving. Local yellowish-buff sandstone.

The front of the fountain-head is carved to show a human head in high relief, with broad, gaping mouth, small lentoid eyes, and thick loosely-waved hair. The back of the stone is hollowed out to receive an inlet pipe. The gaping mouth recalls fountain-heads at Pompeii and elsewhere, but the treatment of the eyes and face reveals strong Celtic influence. The

fountain-head presumably fed a basin in one of the rooms of the bathhouse.

Antonine date.

141 Bolster Fragment   PLATE 35

Prov.: Bearsden, Dunbartonshire, among debris in the Cold Plunge of the annexe bathhouse, during excavation of the fort-site, 1973.

Loc.: Hunterian Museum, University of Glasgow. Inv. no. F.1984.4.

D. J. Breeze, *The Roman Fort at Bearsden* (forthcoming).

The fragment is rather worn.

H.: 0.07 m.; W.: 0.105 m.; D.: 0.08 m.

Relief carving. Local buff sandstone.

The fragment preserves the central part of a bolster from an altar-capital. Around the bolster is a strap decorated with a plain raised boss.

Antonine date.

142 Decorative Border   PLATE 35

Prov.: Bearsden, Dunbartonshire, among debris in the Cold Plunge of the annexe bathhouse, during excavation of the fort-site, 1973.

Loc.: Hunterian Museum, University of Glasgow. Inv. no. F.1984.5.

D. J. Breeze, *The Roman Fort at Bearsden* (forthcoming).

The fragment is worn and slightly chipped.

H.: 0.065 m.; W.: 0.145 m.; D.: 0.04 m.

Relief carving. Local buff sandstone.

The fragment preserves part of the outer border of a sculptured slab decorated with a frieze of leaves and tendrils. Above, is a raised, unidentifiable moulding. The fragment may form part of the outer frame of an *aedicula* (cf. nos. 10, 12) or a gravestone.

Antonine date.

143 Building Stone   PLATE 36

Prov.: Bearsden, Dunbartonshire, among debris overlying the annexe bathhouse, during excavation of the fort-site, 1973.

Loc.: Hunterian Museum, University of Glasgow. Inv. no. F.1984.6.

D. J. Breeze, *The Roman Fort at Bearsden* (forthcoming).

[1] Cf. Espérandieu 3379.

The stone is somewhat worn.

H.: 0.27 m.; W.: 0.185 m.; D.: 0.225 m.

Local buff sandstone. Incised with a rather blunt implement.

On the front face of this dressed building stone is a crude human figure with large head, protruding ears, and deep-set eyes. The legs terminate in short horizontal strokes representing the feet. To the right is a vertical pole from which protrude short lines, angled downwards.

This is perhaps a representation of a soldier holding a military standard. It does, however, have several features in common with various crudely incised 'outline' figures found in civilian as well as military contexts: these are usually held to represent Celtic deities. The 'jug-handle' ears, and the legs formed by extending the vertical outlines of the torso, can be seen, for example, in a figure from Chedworth.[1] The shape of the head, bulbous at the top and tapering slightly towards a squared-off chin, is one favoured in Celtic art. If this is a Celtic deity, the object on the right may be a knotty club or a tree.[2]

Antonine date?

144   Tombstone of Soldier?

Prov.: Castlehill (Bearsden), Dunbartonshire, 'between 1840 and 1850'.

Lost before 1852.

Stuart 1852, p. 310 n. (a); Macdonald 1934, p. 449.

H.: 0.45 m.; W.: 0.305 m.

Relief carving. Type of stone not recorded.

'A small thin slab . . . much worn as if from exposure to weather . . . having sculptured rudely upon it the figure of a Roman soldier, and diamonded on the back by the chisel. Its appearance shows that it was set into some building.'[3]

Antonine date?

145   Distance Slab of the Sixth Legion

PLATE 36

Prov.: Castlehill (Bearsden), Dunbartonshire, on the line of the Antonine Wall, 1698.

Loc.: Hunterian Museum, University of Glasgow. Inv. no. F.6.

T. Tanner, letter to E. Gibson, 1699, in J. Nichols (ed.), *Letters on various Subjects . . . to and from William Nicolson* i, 1809, p. 398, no. 3; R. Fabretti,

Inscriptionum Antiquarum . . . Explicatio et Additamentum 1699, p. 756, no. 620; Sibbald 1707, p. 29 with fig.; Stukeley 1720, p. 9, fig. 3; E. Llwyd, *Philosophical Transactions* xxii, 1700, p. 790, no. 1; W. Camden, *Britannia*, ed. E. Gibson, 1722, p. 1291 with fig.; Gordon 1726, p. 53; Horsley 1732, p. 196, pl. (*Scotland*) iv; Maitland 1757, p. 180; University of Glasgow 1768, pl. iv; Laskey 1813, p. 76, no. 4; Hodgson 1840, p. 267, no. cclxxx; Stuart 1852, p. 314, pl. xvi.2; *CIL* vii, 1132; *EE* ix, p. 628; Macdonald 1897, p. 43, no. 14, pl. v.2; Macdonald 1934, pp. 377–8, no. 8, pl. lxv.1; *RIB* 2196; Keppie 1979, p. 15, no. 8.

Parts of the lower moulding of the die are broken away, and the slab is generally rather worn.

H.: 0.76 m.; W.: 1.49 m.; D.: 0.13 m.

Letter heights: 1–2: 0.045 m.; 3–5: 0.05 m.

Relief carving. Local buff gritstone.

The die is set within raised mouldings, triple-ribbed above and below, but plain to left and right. It is flanked by *peltae*, the horns and central projections of which terminate in rosettes. The *peltae* are carved to represent plumage, and the centre of each is surmounted by a large ivy leaf. The inscription reads: *Imp(eratori) Caesar(i) T(ito) Aelio | Hadriano Antonino | Aug(usto) Pio p(atri) p(atriae) vexillatio | leg(ionis) VI Victr(icis) P(iae) F(idelis) | per m(ilia) p(assuum) IIIDCLXVIs.*

The slab commemorates the completion of $3666\frac{1}{2}$ paces of the Antonine Wall, between Summerston and Castlehill, by a detachment of the Sixth Legion. The other (eastern) end of the sector was marked by no. 138.

Antonine date (probably AD 142–3).

146   Distance Slab of the Twentieth Legion

PLATE 36

Prov.: Castlehill (Bearsden), Dunbartonshire, close to the south lip of the Antonine ditch, 1847.

Loc.: Hunterian Museum, University of Glasgow. Inv. no. F.7.

Wilson 1851, p. 376; Stuart 1852, p. 310, pl. ix.3; *CIL* vii, 1133; *EE* ix, p. 628; J. Buchanan, *TGAS* ser. 1, ii, 1883, pp. 11–28; Macdonald 1897, p. 37, no. 12, pl. xiv.1; A. Gibb, *Scottish Antiquary* xvii, 1902, pp. 72–3; Macdonald 1934, p. 381, no. 9, pl. lxv.2; *RIB* 2197; Keppie 1979, p. 15, no. 9.

---

[1] Ross 1967, p. 185, pl. 60a.   [2] Ibid., pp. 33–8, 172.   [3] Stuart 1852, loc. cit.

The right-hand margin and part of the die were broken off by the plough at the time of discovery.

H.: 0.72 m.; W.: 0.82 m.; D.: 0.13 m.

Letter heights: 1–5: 0.045 m.

The die is enclosed by a double moulding: the outer is plain and the inner decorated with cable-patterns. Below, a boar runs towards the left. The inscription reads: *Imp(eratori) C(aesari)* | *T(ito) Aelio* | *Hadriano* | *Antonino* | *Aug(usto) Pio p(atri) p(atriae)* | *vex(illatio) leg(ionis) XX V(aleriae) V(ictricis)* | *p(er) p(edum) III.*

The slab commemorates the completion of 3000 feet of the Antonine Wall, between Castlehill and Hutcheson Hill, by a detachment of the Twentieth Legion. The other (western) end of the sector was marked by nos. 148–9.

Antonine date (probably AD 142–3).

147 Column Capital · PLATE 36

Prov.: On the west side of Castlehill (Bearsden), Dunbartonshire, 1847.

Loc.: Hunterian Museum, University of Glasgow. Inv. no. F.46.

Wilson 1851, p. 377 with fig.; Stuart 1852, p. 310 n. (*a*), pl. ix.4; Macdonald 1897, p. 91, no. 41, pl. xiv.3; Macdonald 1934, p. 327, pl. li.1; W. Schleiermacher, *Germania* xxxiii, 1960, p. 377.

Parts of the *torus* mouldings are broken away, and the corners of the capital are chipped.

H.: 0.315 m.; W.: 0.425 m.; D.: 0.345 m.

Relief carving. Local buff sandstone.

A channel to receive a horizontal wooden beam has been cut into the top of the capital.

The *abacus* is squared off and its sides ornamented with panels of chevrons, uneven in size. Below the chevrons is a frieze of leaves.

Antonine date.

148 Distance Slab of the Twentieth Legion

PLATE 36

Prov.: Hutcheson Hill, Dunbartonshire, just south of the Antonine Wall, 1865.

Loc.: Taken to Chicago, and there destroyed by fire, 1871. Casts are in the Hunterian Museum, University of Glasgow (Inv. no. F.8), the Museum of

Antiquities (Newcastle), Chesters Museum (Northumberland), and the Grosvenor Museum (Chester).

J. Buchanan, *TGAS* ser 1, ii, 1883, pp. 11–28 (lecture delivered in 1867); *CIL* vii, 1133a: *EE* ix, p. 628; Macdonald 1897, p. 38, no. 13, pl. vi.1; A. Gibb, *Scottish Antiquary* xvii, 1902, pp. 73–7; Macdonald 1934, p. 383, no. 10, pl. lxvi.1; *RIB* 2198; Toynbee 1964, p. 149; Keppie 1979, p. 16, no. 10.

The lower half of the slab was very worn with the loss of some mouldings and a rosette. The fracture across the top left corner probably occurred at the moment of discovery.

H.: 0.67 m.; W.: 0.85 m.; D.: 0.12 m.

Letter heights: 1–8: 0.05 m.

Relief carving. Type of stone not recorded. Two small triangular cramp-holes were set into the top of the slab, and one into each of the sides.

The die was set within triple-beaded mouldings and flanked by ansate panels similarly bordered. Cupids, each carrying a sickle and a bunch of grapes, occupied the *ansae*. The angles between the die and the *ansae* contained rosettes. Below the inscription a boar ran left towards a leafy tree. The inscription read: *Imp(eratori) C(aesari) T(ito)* | *Ael(io) Hadr/iano An/tonino Aug(usto)* | *Pio p(atri) p(atriae) vex(illatio)* | *leg(ionis) XX V(aleriae) V(ictricis)* | *fec(it)* | *p(er) p(edum) III.*

The slab commemorated the completion of 3000 feet of the Antonine Wall, between Castlehill and Hutcheson Hill, by a detachment of the Twentieth Legion. It must have been set up close to no. 149. The other (eastern) end of the sector was marked by no. 146.

Antonine date (probably AD 142–3).

149 Distance Slab of the Twentieth Legion

PLATE 37

Prov.: Hutcheson Hill, Dunbartonshire, on the line of the Antonine Wall, 1969.

Loc.: Hunterian Museum, University of Glasgow. Inv. no. F.1969.22.

A. S. Robertson, *GAJ* i, 1969, p. 1; ead., *Glasgow University Gazette* 61, Dec. 1969, pp. 17–18 with pl.; A. R. Selkirk, *Current Archaeology* Jan. 1970, p. 196; K. A. Steer and E. A. Cormack, *PSAS* ci, 1968–9, p. 121; R. P. Wright, *Britannia* i, 1970, pp. 309–10; *AE* 1971, 255; M. W. C. Hassall, in J. Munby and

M. Henig (eds.), *Roman Life and Art in Britain* ii, 1977, pp. 327–38; Keppie 1979, p. 16, no. 11.

The edges of the slab are broken and chipped, especially at the top right and bottom right corners; the faces and limbs of the sculptured figures have likewise suffered damage, and the legs of the wild boar are partly broken away.

H.: 0.745 m.; W.: 0.95 m.; D.: 0.14 m.

Letter heights: 1–6: 0.035–0.04 m.

Relief carving. Local yellowish-buff sandstone. Set into the top of the slab are two triangular cramp-holes; single cramp-holes are set into the sides.

The slab is carved to represent a triumphal archway, or architectural façade, in which a central arch is flanked by side-niches topped by triangular pediments. Arch and pediments are raised on fluted Corinthian pilasters, the tops of each capital being dentilled. The arch itself consists of a triple-ribbed cornice enriched on the extrados by a series of perforated roundels. The pediments to either side are similarly ribbed and rest upon plain architraves.

Within the central arch stand two figures: to the right a tall female, with a cloak falling over her left shoulder and looped over her left arm. Her hair is neatly piled on top of her head. In her left hand she holds a *patera*, in her right a small laurel wreath which she places in the beak of the eagle atop the standard presented by its bearer. The bowed figure of the bearer occupies the left side of the archway; he is bareheaded, clean-shaven, and faces towards the right, his eyes lowered. His head is shown in very high relief. He grasps with both hands the slender pole of the standard which rests against his left shoulder. He is clad in a tunic and short cloak, his shins are protected by greaves, and on his feet can be discerned the straps of the military sandal. At his right side he wears a short dagger.

The side-panels are each occupied by a sturdy native warrior kneeling in subjection, hands tied behind his back. The hair of each figure is indicated by rigid lines, perhaps intended to represent the limed hair of Celtic warriors. The naked figure in the left-hand niche is clean-shaven; his head is tilted upwards to the right, surveying the central scene. The right-hand niche is occupied by a similar, but bearded, figure, seemingly in a loincloth, who looks upwards towards the left. Behind the heads of the captives are circular panels, probably shields, bearing some parts of the inscription.

The podium is divided into three sections corresponding to the sculptured scenes above. Centrally placed is a wild boar running towards the right. The panels to left and right are flanked by *peltae*. The inscription, distributed wherever room was available amid the sculptured figures, reads: *Im[p(eratori)] C(aesari) | T(ito) Ae(lio) | Hadri|ano | Anto|nino | Aug(usto) | Pio p(atri) p(atriae) | vex(illatio) leg(ionis) | XX V(aleriae) V(ictricis) | fec(it) | p(er) p(edum) III*.

The slab commemorates the completion of 3000 feet of the Antonine Wall by a detachment of the Twentieth Legion. It was presumably set up close to no. 148. The other (eastern) end of the sector was marked by no. 146. The sculptured scenes emphasize the victory of the Roman army. The defeated tribesmen look on as the eagle, representative of the legion, receives a fitting reward. The tall female figure may be Victory (though she lacks wings and one of her normal attributes, a palm frond) or Britannia, personification of the newly enlarged province, who congratulates the army on its successes.

Antonine date (probably AD 142–3).

150 Distance Slab of the Sixth Legion

PLATE 37

Prov.: Braidfield, Dunbartonshire, on the line of the Antonine Wall, 1812.

Loc.: Hunterian Museum, University of Glasgow. Inv. no. F.9.

Glasgow Courier 7 July 1812; Laskey 1813, p. 77; Hodgson 1840, p. 271, no. ccxc; Stuart 1852, p. 300, pl. vii.7; Macdonald 1897, pp. 27–8, no. 5, pl. iii.1; Macdonald 1934, p. 384, no. 11, pl. lxvi.2; *RIB* 2200; Toynbee 1964, p. 149; Keppie 1979, p. 17, no. 12.

Parts of the outer mouldings are chipped and worn.

H.: 0.76 m.; W.: 1.19 m.; D.: 0.18 m.

Letter heights: 1–6: 0.03 m.

Relief carving. Local whitish-buff sandstone.

The inscribed panel is held aloft by two winged Victories flanked by Mars and Valour. The die itself is enclosed within triple mouldings and flanked by *peltae*, the terminals of which end in plain roundels, and the outlines of which are emphasized by herringbone-patterns. The two Victories, their hair piled high on their heads and their draperies billowing, each rest one foot on a globe. Mars is equipped with a triple-plumed helmet, moulded cuirass, and cloak falling from his right shoulder. He rests his left hand on a shield and holds a spear in his right. Valour, in a short tunic with an overfold, which leaves her right breast bare in Amazon fashion, holds in her right hand a *vexillum* inscribed *Virt(us) Aug(usti)* and in her left a sheathed sword reversed, the scabbard of which rests in the crook of her arm. On her head is a plumed helmet. The inscription reads: *Imp(eratori) C(aesari) T(ito) Aelio Hadr/iano Antonino Aug(usto) | p(atri) p(atriae) vex(illatio) leg(ionis) VI | Victric(i)s P(iae) F(idelis) | opus valli p(edum) | (tria milia) CCXL f(ecit)*.

The slab commemorates the completion of 3240 feet of the Antonine Wall, between Hutcheson Hill and Braidfield, by a detachment of the Sixth Legion.

Antonine date (probably AD 142–3).

151 Statue of a Water Nymph   PLATE 37

Prov.: Duntocher, Dunbartonshire, in the fort bathhouse, 1775.

Loc.: Hunterian Museum, University of Glasgow. Inv. no. F.44.

J. Knox, *A View of the British Empire, more especially Scotland* 1785, p. 611 n.; Stuart 1852, p. 365, pl. xv.3; Macdonald 1897, p. 93, no. 44, pl. xii.2; Macdonald 1934, p. 330, pp. 444–5, pl. lxxvii.5; A. S. Robertson, *An Antonine Fort: Golden Hill, Duntocher* 1957, pp. 4–5.

The statue is broken into three parts, and the fragments are rather worn.

H.: 0.58 m.; W.: 0.21 m.; D.: 0.19 m.

Carved in the round. Local buff sandstone.

A female figure, naked to the waist and with wavy hair falling to her shoulders, stands facing the front, holding a pierced oval shell angled slightly upwards. On her upper arms are a pair of narrow armlets.

The statue, which probably represents a water nymph, served as a gurget in the fort bathhouse. Water must have poured out through the centre of the shell, perhaps into a basin. The folds on her lower draperies may have been intended to represent the flowing waters. The stiff pose of the figure, the elongated neck, the patterning of the hair, shell, and

draperies, the lentoid eyes, and wedge-shaped nose are all suggestive of Celtic workmanship.[1]

Antonine date.

152 Distance Slab of the Second Legion
PLATE 37

Prov.: Unknown, but located by reasonable conjecture at Duntocher, Dunbartonshire, on the line of the Antonine Wall; before 1845.

Loc.: Hunterian Museum, University of Glasgow. Inv. no. F.10.

Stuart 1852, p. 298, pl. viii.1; *CIL* vii, 1138; *EE* ix, p. 629; Macdonald 1897, p. 30, no. 7, pl. xiii.1; A. Gibb, *Scottish Antiquary* xvi, 1902, pp. 62–6; Macdonald 1934, p. 386, no. 12, pl. lxvii.1; *RIB* 2203; Toynbee 1964, p. 149; Keppie 1979, p. 17, no. 13.

Some damage has been sustained to the right side of the slab; one of the rosettes is all but lost.

H.: 0.5 m.; W.: 0.71 m.; D.: 0.18 m.

Letter heights: 1, 3: 0.04 m.; 2, 4: 0.025 m.

Relief carving. Local buff sandstone. Two large, triangular cramp-holes have been set into the top of the slab.

The die is enclosed within a double frame; the outer is plain and the inner is decorated with acanthus-leaf designs. The die is flanked by *peltae*, the horns of which terminate in griffin-heads with ropes or torcs around their necks. Above, a capricorn with twisted tail swims towards the left; below, a pegasus with streaming tail gallops in the same direction. The four corners of the stone are occupied by rosettes. The inscription reads: *leg(io) | II | Aug(usta) f(ecit) | p(edum) IIIICXL*.

The slab commemorates the completion of 4140 feet of the Antonine Wall, between Braidfield and Duntocher, by a detachment of the Second Legion. The names and titles of the emperor Antoninus have been omitted.

Antonine date (probably AD 142–3).

153 Altar to Jupiter Optimus Maximus
PLATE 38

Prov.: Easter Duntinglennan Farm, Dunbartonshire, near the fort-site at Duntocher, 1829.

Loc.: Hunterian Museum, University of Glasgow. Inv. no. F.32.

---

[1] Cf. Phillips 1977, no. 35 for a similar subject, skilfully executed in the Graeco-Roman manner.

Stuart 1852, p. 300; *CIL* vii, 1134; Macdonald 1897, p. 32, no. 9, pl. xv.2; Macdonald 1934, p. 434, no. 53; *RIB* 2201.

The altar is very badly weathered. The inscription is now almost illegible.

H.: 0.635 m.; W.: 0.315 m.; D.: 0.32 m.

Letter heights: 1: 0.045 m.

Relief carving. Local buff sandstone.

The sides of the shaft are decorated with sacrificial implements; on the left is a jug and a knife, on the right is a handle-less *patera*. The inscription reads: *I(ovi) O(ptimo) [M(aximo) | ....*

Antonine date.

## 154	Distance Slab of the Second Legion

PLATE 38

Prov.: Carleith, Dunbartonshire, on the line of the Antonine Wall, before 1699.

Loc.: Hunterian Museum, University of Glasgow. Inv. no. F.12.

T. Tanner, letter to E. Gibson, 1699, in J. Nichols (ed.), *Letters on various Subjects . . . to and from William Nicolson* i, 1809, p. 338, no. 4; Stukeley 1720, p. 9, fig. iii; Gordon 1726, p. 51, pl. x.1; Horsley 1732, p. 195, pl. (*Scotland*) ii; University of Glasgow 1768, pl. ii; Laskey 1813, p. 76, no. 2; Hodgson 1840, p. 268, no. cclxxxvi; Stuart 1852, p. 296, pl. viii.6; *CIL* vii, 1136; *EE* ix, p. 628; Macdonald 1897, p. 25, no. 4, pl. ii.3; A. Gibb, *Scottish Antiquary* xv, 1901, p. 86; ibid., xvi, 1902, p. 191; Macdonald 1934, p. 387, no. 14, pl. lxviii.1; *RIB* 2204; Keppie 1979, p. 18, no. 14.

The outer moulding is slightly damaged.

H.: 0.53 m.; W.: 0.63 m.; D.: 0.16 m.

Letter heights: 1–3: 0.025 m.; 4: 0.05 m.; 5: 0.025 m.; 6: 0.025–0.05 m.; 7: 0.025–0.035 m.

Relief carving. Local buff sandstone. A small triangular cramp-hole has been set into the top of the slab.

The die is enclosed within a border of cable-patterns, and flanked by *peltae*, the horns of which terminate in griffin-heads with ropes or torcs around their necks. The central projections end in plain bosses. Above, a capricorn swims left; below, a pegasus gallops in the same direction. The four corners of the slab are occupied by elaborate double rosettes. The inscrip-

tion, partly contained within the die and partly crushed into the vacant spaces to left and right of the capricorn, reads: *Imp(eratori) Anton(ino) | Aug(usto) Pio | p(atri) p(atriae) | leg(io) | II | Aug(usta) | f(ecit) p(edum) IIICCLXXI.*

The slab commemorates the completion of 3271 feet of the Antonine Wall, between Carleith and Duntocher, by the Second Legion. In design this slab closely resembles no. 152 which commemorates the completion of the adjacent sector by the same legion, but it is less well executed.

Antonine date (probably AD 142–3).

## 155	Distance Slab of the Twentieth Legion

PLATE 38

Prov.: Near Old Kilpatrick, Dunbartonshire, on the line of the Antonine Wall, before 1695.

Loc.: Hunterian Museum, University of Glasgow. Inv. no. F.14.

Sibbald 1707, p. 52 with fig.; Stukeley 1720, pp. 8–9, no. 2; W. Camden, *Britannia*, ed. E. Gibson, 1722, p. 1215; Gordon 1726, p. 62; Horsley 1732, p. 197, pl. (*Scotland*) vi; University of Glasgow 1768, pl. vi; Hodgson 1840, p. 267, pl. cclxxxii; Stuart 1852, p. 289, pl. vii.2; *CIL* vii, 1142; *EE* ix, p. 629; Macdonald 1897, p. 23, no. 3, pl. vii.2; A. Gibb, *Scottish Antiquary* xv, 1901, pp. 205–6; ibid., xvi, 1902, pp. 54–9; Macdonald 1934, p. 390, no. 16, pl. lxix.1; *RIB* 2206; Keppie 1979, p. 19, no. 16.

Two adjoining fragments preserve the right side-panel and a substantial part of the die. The smaller fragment was illustrated by Sibbald and mentioned by Horsley, but has escaped the notice of all subsequent commentators. Both fragments are very worn, and the face of the Cupid may have been deliberately defaced.

H.: 0.66 m.; W.: 0.62 m.; D.: 0.1 m. When complete the slab probably had a width of 0.88 m.

Letter heights: 1: 0.035 m.; 2–3: 0.04 m.; 4–6: 0.035 m.

Relief carving. Local yellowish-buff sandstone. A small triangular cramp-hole is set into the top of the slab; there would have been another further to the left.

The die is enclosed within triple mouldings, and flanked to the right, and presumably also to the left, by *ansae* similarly bordered. The surviving *ansa* contains a Cupid, walking towards the left, and carrying a bunch of grapes in his left hand. Above and below the *ansa* are rosettes. The inscription reads: [*I*]*mp(eratori) C(aesari) T(ito) Ae(lio)* | [*H*]*adriano* | [*A*]*ntonino* | [*A*]*ug(usto) Pio p(atri) p(atriae)* | [*vex(illatio) l*]*eg(ionis) XX V(aleriae) V(ictricis)* | [*p(er) p(edum) IIIIC*]*DXI.* [*fec(it)*].

The slab commemorates the completion of 4411 feet of the Antonine Wall, between Dalnotter and Old Kilpatrick, by a detachment of the Twentieth Legion. The western end of the sector was marked by no. 156. The surviving part of this slab is identical in design to no. 148 above, so that its overall layout is clear. Space is available below the inscription (as on no. 148) for a boar emblem.

Antonine date (probably AD 142-3).

156 Distance Slab of the Twentieth Legion

PLATE 38

Prov.: Ferrydyke (Old Kilpatrick), Dunbartonshire, at the western terminus of the Antonine Wall, before 1684.

Loc.: Hunterian Museum, University of Glasgow. Inv. no. F.15.

W. Camden, *Britannia*, ed. E. Gibson, 1695, pp. 1101-2 with fig.; Sibbald 1697, p. 207; 1707, pp. 49-50; Stukeley 1720, p. 10, no. 6; Gordon 1726, p. 51, pl. ix.1; Horsley 1732, p. 194, pl. (*Scotland*) i; Maitland 1757, p. 182-3; University of Glasgow 1768, pl. i; Laskey 1813, p. 76, no. 1; Hodgson 1840, p. 268, no. cclxxxvii; Stuart 1852, p. 292, pl. vii.1; *CIL* vii, 1141; *EE* ix, p. 629; Macdonald 1897, p. 20, no. 1, pl. i.1; A. Gibb, *Scottish Antiquary* xv, 1901, pp. 199-200; Macdonald 1934, p. 390, no. 17, pl. lxix.2; *RIB* 2208; Toynbee 1964, p. 149; Keppie 1979, p. 19, no. 17.

The stone is worn and chipped at the edges. The face of the reclining figure and the wreath have suffered damage.

H.: 0.69 m.; W.: 0.73 m.; D.: 0.12 m.

Letter heights: 1-6: 0.03 m.; 7: 0.035 m.

Relief carving. Local buff sandstone. A single, almost square cramp-hole has been set into the top of the slab at its gable-angle.

The slab takes the form of a temple-façade flanked by Corinthian pilasters. The pediment is enclosed by a plain cornice and is set directly on the pilasters, between which is a reclining Victory. Her hair is piled elaborately on top of her head, and she rests her left elbow on a globe on which criss-cross bands can be discerned. She is naked to the thighs, with drapery covering her legs. In her left hand she holds a palm frond and in her right a large laurel wreath, within which the name and titles of the legion are inscribed. The podium is carved to show an elongated panel flanked by *ansae* surmounted by rosettes. Within the panel, a boar, placed slightly left of the centre, runs towards the left. The inscription, which is divided among the pediment, wreath, and podium, reads: *Imp(eratori) C(aesari)* | *T(ito) Ae(lio) Hadria*/*no Antonino Aug(usto) Pio p(atri) p(atriae)* | *vex(illatio)* | *leg(ionis) XX* | *V(aleriae) V(ictricis) fec(it)* | *p(er) p(edum) IIIICDXI.*

The slab commemorates completion of 4411 feet of the Antonine Wall, between Dalnotter and Old Kilpatrick, by a detachment of the Twentieth Legion. The other (eastern) end was matched by no. 155. A reclining, half-naked Victory is unusual and the mason may have used as his model one of the river deities or water-nymphs shown on coins or on the sculptured reliefs of this period.

Antonine date (probably AD 142-3).

157 Distance Slab of the Twentieth Legion

PLATE 38

Prov.: Unknown, but donated to Glasgow University by the proprietor of Cochno House, Duntocher, before 1695. It must belong to one of the two sectors of the Antonine Wall west of Castlehill completed by the Twentieth Legion.

Loc.: Hunterian Museum, University of Glasgow. Inv. no. F.11.

Gordon 1726, p. 61, pl. ix.3; Horsley 1732, p. 196, pl. (*Scotland*) v; University of Glasgow 1768, pl. v; Hodgson 1840, p. 267, no. cclxxxi; Stuart 1852, p. 299, pl. viii.5; *CIL* vii, 1137; Macdonald 1897, p. 28, no. 6, pl. xiii.2; A. Gibb, *Scottish Antiquary* xvii, 1902, pp. 77-8; Macdonald 1934, p. 387, no. 13, pl. lxvii.2; *RIB* 2199; Keppie 1979, p. 19, no. 18.

Parts of the outer moulding at the bottom right, top right, and gable-angles are broken away.

H.: 0.56 m.; W.: 0.75 m.; D.: 0.115 m.

Letter heights: 1-6: 0.05 m.

Relief carving. Local buff sandstone. A small triangular cramp-hole is set into the gable-angle of the slab.

The five-sided slab is bordered by a double mould-ing, the outer of which is plain and the inner decora-ted with cable-patterns. Below the inscription, a boar runs towards the right. The inscription reads: *Imp(eratori) C(aesari) | T(ito) Ae(lio) Hadriano | Antonino Aug(usto) | Pio p(atri) p(atriae) vex(illatio) leg(ionis) | XXV(aleriae) V(ictricis) fec(it) | p(edum)* ...

The slab commemorates the completion of a sector of the Antonine Wall, either that between Castlehill and Hutcheson Hill, or that between Dalnotter and Old Kilpatrick, but the number of feet has not been inserted. There is no reason to suppose that the slab was a 'waster'.

Antonine date (probably AD 142–3).

158   Distance Slab of the Twentieth Legion
PLATE 39

Prov.: On the line of the Antonine Wall, at a point unknown, before 1607.

Loc.: Hunterian Museum, University of Glasgow. Inv. no. F.1.

Anonymus Germanus, BM MS *Cotton Julius* F VI, f. 351; W. Camden, ibid., f. 295; id., *Britannia* 1607, p. 699 with fig.; R. Sibbald, *Introductio ad historiam rerum a Romanis gestarum* 1706, p. 52; 1707, p. 50; Stukeley 1720, MS gloss at p. 10 with fig.; Gordon 1726, p. 62, pl. xii.2; Horsley 1732, p. 204, pl. (*Scotland*), xxvi; University of Glasgow 1768, pl. xiv.1; Hodgson 1840, p. 263, no. cclxi; Stuart 1852, p. 364, pl. xv.8; *CIL* vii, 1143; *EE* vii, 1094; *EE* ix, p. 630; *ILS* 2482; Macdonald 1897, p. 46, no. 16, pl. iv.1; A. Gibb, *Scottish Antiquary* xvii, 1902, pp. 78–81; Macdonald 1934, p. 365, no. 2, pl. lxii.1; Toynbee 1964, pp. 149–50; *RIB* 2173; Keppie 1979, p. 12, no. 2.

The slab is broken horizontally across the die. The surface is badly pitted and several letters near the break are damaged. Traces remain of gold and black paint applied *c.*1600 to the border and the letters.

H.: 0.87 m.; W.: 0.97 m.; D.: 0.105 m.

Letter heights: 1: 0.06 m.; 2–7: 0.05 m.

Relief carving. Local buff sandstone. Two small tri-angular cramp-holes are set into the top face of the slab.

The die is set within a double raised moulding, and flanked by *peltae* carved to represent plumage; the

horns terminate in griffin-heads with staring eyes and gaping beaks. The *peltae* are surmounted by four-petalled rosettes, and the central projections are ornamented with circular studs. Above and below the die are horizontal bands of leafy spirals. The in-scription reads: *Imp(eratori) Caesari | T(ito) Aelio Hadri|ano Antonino | Aug(usto) Pio p(atri) p(atriae) | vexillatio | leg(ionis) XX Val(eriae) Vic(tricis) f(ecit) | per mil(ia) p(assuum) III.*

The slab records the completion of 3000 paces of the Antonine Wall by a detachment of the Twentieth Legion. The sector has not been located, but must lie in the eastern half of the Wall line.

Antonine date (probably AD 142–3).

159   Sculptured Panel
PLATE 39

Prov.: Unknown, before *c.*1771. The panel probably derived from an Antonine Wall site.

Loc.: Hunterian Museum, University of Glasgow. Inv. no. F.42.

University of Glasgow 1768 (*Suppl. c.*1771), pl. xxxii; Laskey 1813, p. 77, no. 32; Stuart 1852, p. 365, pl. xv.4; Macdonald 1897, p. 93, no. 43, pl. xii.1; Macdonald 1934, p. 448, pl. lxxvi.5.

The tablet is broken into four fragments, and the edges of each are much worn; the outer moulding is broken away at the bottom left-hand corner.

H.: 0.45 m.; W.: 0.45 m.; D.: 0.085 m.

Relief carving. Local buff sandstone.

Within a plain moulding a man, his head turned towards the front and his back bent almost double, walks towards the left, leaning on a staff. Behind him a smaller male figure, clad in a tunic or *bracae* reaching to his knees, sits with his legs towards the left. He may be pushing at the man to assist his progress or perhaps pulling him back. The face of the smaller figure is almost totally lost, but he too seems to be facing the front.

The scene has been supposed to represent Youth and Old Age, but it cannot be said that any satisfac-tory interpretation has yet been offered. The slab was perhaps one of a sequence of panels, decorating a sepulchral monument.[1] Alternatively (and perhaps more probably) the content is obscene,[2] and the panel derived from a shrine to a local fertility cult.

Antonine date.

---

[1] Cf. Espérandieu 5040.   [2] Cf. F. Oswald, *Index of Figure-Types on Terra Sigillata* ('*Samian Ware*') 1936–7, pl. xc.

PART III

SCOTLAND NORTH OF THE ANTONINE WALL

SCOTLAND NORTH OF THE ANTONINE WALL

160 Uninscribed Altar PLATE 39

Prov.: Camelon, Stirlingshire, c.1903.

Loc.: National Museum of Antiquities of Scotland, Edinburgh. Inv. no. FX 336.

PSAS xxxviii, 1903–4, p. 149.

The altar is worn and the corners of the capital, shaft, and base are damaged. It has a pronounced list to the right.

H.: 0.39 m.; W.: 0.145 m.; D.: 0.145 m.

Relief carving. Local buff sandstone.

Two bands of cable-patterns on the front of the capital are the only decoration.

1st/2nd century AD.

161 Statue PLATE 39

Prov.: Camelon, Stirlingshire, c.1905.[1]

Loc. National Museum of Antiquities of Scotland, Edinburgh. Inv. no. FX 341.

Unpublished.

The head, arms, and lower legs are lost, and the genitals are broken away. The torso is worn and pitted.

H.: 0.46 m.; W.: 0.26 m.; D.: 0.17 m.

Carved in the round. Local buff sandstone. There is some evidence of reworking: initially the draperies probably extended to the figure's left hip.[2]

A muscular male figure, naked except for draperies over the left shoulder, stands erect. When complete, the statue probably measured c.0.9 m. in height, and so was about half life-size. The lower abdomen and navel have been carved (or perhaps reworked) to represent a human head, almost circular in shape,

with a triangular gaping mouth and wedge-shaped nose.

The statue may have represented a Romano-Celtic deity. The placing of a head close to the reproductive organs symbolized fertility in Celtic art.[3]

1st/2nd century AD.

162 Statue Fragment PLATE 40

Prov.: Camelon, Stirlingshire, during excavation of the fort-site, 1900.

Loc.: National Museum of Antiquities of Scotland, Edinburgh. Inv. no. FX 312.

Anderson 1901, p. 414.

The fragment shows the front part of a sandalled left foot resting on a plinth.

H.: 0.095 m.; W.: 0.11 m.; D.: 0.085 m.

Relief carving. Local buff sandstone.

The sandal is held in place by thongs attached to a central strap. The foot evidently belonged to a statue of about half life-size.

1st/2nd century AD.

163 Building Stone PLATE 40

Prov.: Camelon, Stirlingshire, during excavation of the fort-site, 1900.

Loc.: National Museum of Antiquities of Scotland, Edinburgh. Inv. no. FX 309.

Anderson 1901, p. 413, fig. 53.

H.: 0.16 m.; W.: 0.28 m.; D.: 0.3 m.

Incised. Local buff sandstone.

Between two vertical palm branches is a *vexillum* on a slender pole with a double handle near its base. The

---

[1] The torso is catalogued in the National Museum of Antiquities along with material recovered during excavation of the fort-site in 1900; but the published report (see *PSAS* xxxv, 1900–1, pp. 329–417) omits mention of it. The torso appears on a photograph dated 1905, formerly in the collection of Mr Mungo Buchanan, and now at Falkirk Museum. The photograph shows the torso being examined by a group of local antiquarians, apparently at Falkirk or Camelon, so that its discovery seems likely to post-date the excavations by several years.

[2] We are grateful to Dr Susan Walker for her comments.

[3] Ross 1967, p. 93 n. 3.

vexillum-panel is divided into three parts by two vertical lines.

It is possible that the vertical strokes were intended as the numerals of the Second Legion.

1st/2nd century AD (probably Antonine date?).

164   Building Stone   PLATE 40

Prov.: Camelon, Stirlingshire, during excavation of the south annexe, in the stone bottoming of an Antonine II road, 1976.

Loc.: At present with the excavator, Dr V. A. Maxfield. To be deposited in Falkirk Museum.

V. A. Maxfield, in D. J. Breeze (ed.), *Roman Scotland: Some Recent Excavations* 1979, p. 31.

Only the right-hand half of the stone survives. It was broken horizontally into two parts, at the moment of discovery. Part of the outer right-hand moulding is broken away and the details of the figure are much worn.

H.: 0.185 m.; W.: 0.94 m.; D.: 0.125 m.

Relief carving. Local buff sandstone.

Within a doubled raised moulding, a winged Victory faces the front. Her draperies fall to the knee but she is apparently naked above the waist. Her right foot rests upon a globe. In her left hand she holds a palm branch which partly overlies the outer moulding.

It is probable that the missing portion of the stone bore an inscription, perhaps contained within a wreath or panel supported by a pair of Victory-figures.

Antonine date (probably within the date-range AD 142–57)?

165   Sculptured Slabs   PLATE 40

Prov.: On the outer facing stones of the Roman monument known as Arthur's O'on, Larbert, Stirlingshire, 3 km north of the Antonine Wall; first reported 1527.

Now lost. Arthur's O'on was dismantled in 1743 to provide materials for the building of a mill-dam.

H. Boece, *Scotorum Historiae* 1527, *Lib*. iii, fol. xxv; Anonymous Traveller, 1697, in Historical MSS Commission, *xiiith Report* (= *Portland Papers* ii),

1893, p. 56; R. Sibbald, letter of 1699 to E. Llywd—see F. J. Haverfield, *PSAS* xliv, 1909–10, p. 326; Sibbald 1707, pp. 42–6 with fig. at p. 52; Stukeley 1720, *passim*; Gordon 1726, pp. 24–32; Horsley 1732, pp. 174–5; Maitland 1757, pp. 208–9; Stuart 1852, pp. 183–4; K. A. Steer, *Arch. J.* cxv, 1958, pp. 99–110; RCAHMS 1963, i, p. 118, no. 126; I. G. Brown, *Antiquity* xlviii, 1974, pp. 283–8; K. A. Steer, *GAJ* iv, 1976, pp. 90–2; T. W. Tatton-Brown, *Britannia* xi, 1980, pp. 340–3.

No measurements given for sculptural decoration.

Relief carving. Local sandstone.

Several early antiquaries reported seeing sculptured reliefs on the outside of the domed monument, especially above its arched doorway, but their descriptions differ, and no drawings have survived. Boece and Sibbald noticed one or more eagles, or eagle-heads, while the 'Anonymous Traveller of 1697' and Sibbald report a winged figure, whom they interpreted as Victory. D. Buchanan (cited by Gordon) describes two military standards, having between them an eagle with outstretched wings.

Arthur's O'on has been interpreted as a Roman temple or victory monument, commemorating the campaigns of Agricola, Lollius Urbicus, or even Severus. A dedicatory panel might be expected above the door, but how the various sculptures were positioned remains uncertain. A brass finger, perhaps a remnant of a statue which stood on or in the monument, is also reported.[1]

1st/3rd centuries AD.

166   Mortar Fragment   PLATE 40

Prov.: Ardoch, Perthshire, during excavation of the fort-site, 1896–7.

Loc.: National Museum of Antiquities of Scotland, Edinburgh. Inv. no. FQ 188.

Anderson 1898, p. 467.

The fragment, preserving a segment of the rim of a heavy stone vessel, perhaps a mortar, shows a human head.

H.: 0.07 m.; W.: 0.11 m.; D.: 0.06 m.

Incised. Local buff sandstone.

The head may have been one of several decorating the rim of the vessel. Its crude features are Celtic in

[1] K. A. Steer, *GAJ* iv, 1976, p. 90–2.

style: the round or open mouth, especially, is characteristic of heads decorating Celtic pots from both pre-Roman and Roman times.[1]

1st/2nd centuries AD?

167 Fragments of Commemorative Slab

PLATE 41

Prov.: Ardoch, Perthshire, during excavation of the fort-site, 1896–7.

Loc.: National Museum of Antiquities of Scotland, Edinburgh. Inv. nos. FQ 185, 186.

Anderson 1898, pp. 466–7, fig. 18. Fragment a: *EE* ix, 1248a; *RIB* 2211.

The two fragments (which do not adjoin) derive from the decorative border of a commemorative slab.

a: H.: 0.165 m.; W.: 0.1 m.; D.: 0.09 m. b: H.: 0.12 m.; W.: 0.165 m.; D.: 0.08 m.

Relief carving. Local buff sandstone.

The outer border of the slab was ornamented with a frieze of leaves and fruit clusters. The inscription (on fragment a) reads: *Im[p(eratori)......*

Antonine date?

168 Fragments of Commemorative Slab(s)

PLATE 41

Prov.: Ardoch, Perthshire, during excavation of the fort-site, 1896–7.

Loc.: National Museum of Antiquities of Scotland, Edinburgh. Inv. nos. FQ 189, 190, 191, 192, 194, 195.

Anderson 1898, 466–7.

The fragments, here designated a–f, preserve parts of the ornamentation, perhaps the decorated borders, of one or more sculptured slabs.

a: H.: 0.18 m.; W.: 0.1 m.; D.: 0.095 m. b: H.: 0.12 m.; W.: 0.09 m.; D.: 0.1 m. c: H.: 0.1 m.; W.: 0.08 m.; D.: 0.095 m. d: H.: 0.195 m.; W.: 0.114 m.; D.: 0.085 m. e: H.: 0.07 m.; W.: 0.09 m.; D.: 0.04 m. f: H.: 0.09 m.; W.: 0.075 m.; D.: 0.04 m.

Relief carving. Local reddish-buff sandstone.

Fragments a, b, and f show fruit clusters and foliage, some rather worn. Two others, c and e, show narrow

mouldings, of uncertain significance (Anderson identified c as showing 'part of a human limb'). On d can be seen a more elaborate zigzag ornament. The tablet was evidently inscribed, as the single bar of a letter, perhaps L, can be seen on b.[2]

1st/2nd century AD (probably Antonine date?).

169 Fragment of Sculptured Slab

PLATE 41

Prov.: Ardoch, Perthshire, during excavation of the fort-site, 1896–7.

Loc.: National Museum of Antiquities, Edinburgh. Inv. no. FQ 187.

Anderson 1898, p. 467.

H.: 0.12 m.; W.: 0.15 m.; D.: 0.08 m.

Relief carving. Buff sandstone.

The fragment shows a large leaf with prominent ribbing.

1st/2nd century AD (probably Antonine date?).

170 Fragment of Statue?

PLATE 41

Prov.: Possibly Ardoch, Perthshire, during excavation of the fort-site, 1896–7.

Loc.: National Museum of Antiquities of Scotland, Edinburgh. Inv. no. ?FQ 189.

Unpublished.

The fragment may preserve the upper part of the head of a small statue, of about quarter life-size.

H.: 0.06 m.; W.: 0.1 m.; D.: 0.125 m.

Carved in the round. Local buff sandstone.

To either side of a thick central stem are sets of wavy lines, perhaps intended as hair or the feathers of a plumed helmet.

1st/2nd century AD.

171 Fragment of Commemorative Slab

PLATE 41

Prov.: Carpow, Perthshire, during excavation of the east gate of the vexillation-fortress, 1964.

Loc.: Dundee Museums and Art Galleries, Inv. no. 1969-264(1).

---

[1] For an applied human head on a pottery fragment from Worcester, see M. J. Green, *The Religions of Civilian Roman Britain*, Oxford, 1976 (*British Archaeological Reports* 24), p. 172,

pl. xxviif.

[2] A further fragment from Ardoch, bearing parts of two incised letters, may belong to the same slab (Inv. no. FQ 193).

R. P. Wright, *PSAS* xcv, 1963-4, pp. 202-5, pl. x.1; id., *JRS* lv, 1965, pp. 223-4, no. 10, pl. xix.1-2; H. Coutts, *Tayside before History* 1971, p. 81, no. 187a(1); R. P. Wright, *Acta of the Fifth Epigraphic Congress 1967* 1971, pp. 293-7, pl. 26; id., *Britannia* v, 1974, pp. 289-92.

A large fragment preserves the greater part of the sculptured left-hand side panel of a massive commemorative slab and a small area of the die. Four other fragments (not illustrated), all inscribed, were also recovered.[1] Some letters show signs of the original red paint.

H.: 0.9 m.; W.: 0.86 m.; D.: 0.185 m.

Letter heights: 1-2: 0.14 m. Secondary inscription: 1: 0.03 m.

Relief carving. Local red sandstone.

The horns of the surviving left-hand *pelta* terminate in bird-heads and the central projection in a cone. To the left of the upper terminal is a winged Victory, with a palm frond held vertically in her left hand. She probably held a wreath in her right. Her draperies reach to the ankles and she is poised rather uncertainly on a small globe. Much of the upper half of her body is broken away. On the right, a capricorn with horns and a twisted fish-tail moves towards the left. Below the central projection are two confronting pegasi and below them the head and wings, possibly of an eagle (so R. P. Wright) but more probably of a second Victory. To accommodate this figure the lower *pelta*-horn has been substantially curtailed. The inscription, which probably consisted of four lines of text, reads: [*I*]*mp(erator) e*[*t Dominus N(oster) M(arcus) Aur(elius) Antoninus* | *Piu*]*s F*[*el(ix)* ....A secondary inscription, below the lower *pelta*-horn, reads: ...]*p fe*[*c(it)*].

The slab, presumably erected above the east gate of the fortress to record its construction, was the work of craftsmen of the Second Legion, as the capricorn and pegasi indicate.

Severan date (probably AD 211-12).

172   Fragment of Commemorative Slab

PLATE 42

Prov.: Carpow, Perthshire, during excavation of the south gate of the vexillation-fortress, 1970.

Loc.: Dundee Museums and Art Galleries. Inv. no. 1971-430.

R. P. Wright and M. W. C. Hassall, *Britannia* ii, 1971, p. 292, no. 15(a), pl. xl; H. Coutts, *Tayside before History* 1971, p. 82, no. 187e(1).

The fragment preserves the top right-hand corner of a massive slab on which the die was flanked by *peltae* set within plain mouldings. Two other small fragments found at the south gate may belong with this slab.[2]

H.: 0.5 m.; W.: 0.47 m.; D.: 0.22 m.

Relief carving. Local red sandstone. Set into the top of the slab is a dovetail cramp-hole.

The surviving right hand *pelta* was carved to represent plumage with the upper horn terminating in an eagle-head. Above the terminal is a vine-leaf and a grape cluster suspended from a horizontal branch. To the right of the *pelta* a raised circular moulding, decorated with crudely incised cable-patterns, may have been intended to represent a laurel wreath. Below it a tendril terminates in an ivy leaf.

The slab when complete must have been erected above the south gate. The motifs employed do not themselves allow the legion responsible to be identified, but one of the small inscribed fragments has been thought to mention the Second Legion which also built the east gate (see no. 171 above).

Severan date (probably AD 211-12).

---

[1] *JRS* lv, 1965, p. 223, no. 10; ibid., lvi, 1966, p. 219, no. 7a-c.   [2] *Britannia* ii, 1971, p. 292, no. 15(b) and 15(c).

APPENDIX

I T is appropriate here to mention briefly a few stones which either do not belong to Scotland, or are of dubious antiquity.

ALIENA

(a) Five Sculptured Reliefs

Abbotsford House, Melrose, Roxburghshire.

Five reliefs, showing Jupiter, Apollo, Mercury, Mars, and Venus standing within niches, are built into the garden wall at Abbotsford House. They were found at the fort-site of Old Penrith, Cumbria, in 1813, and brought to Abbotsford by Sir Walter Scott. See F. J. Haverfield, *CW* N.S. xiii, 1913, p. 194 with figures; RCAHMS 1956, ii, p. 301.

(b) Building Stone

Birrens (*Blatobulgium*), Dumfriesshire.

A building stone, inscribed with the names and titles of the Sixth Legion set within a laurel wreath, was purchased by Sir John Clerk of Pennicuik at Bowness on Solway in 1739. It passed to the National Museum of Antiquities, Edinburgh, in 1857, and was catalogued by E. Hübner (*CIL* vii, 1075) under Birrens with other stones from the Clerk collection. Essential bibliography at *RIB* 2061, where the attribution to Bowness is confirmed.

(c) Tombstone

Birrens (*Blatobulgium*), Dumfriesshire.

A gabled tombstone with a full-length representation of the deceased was first reported by Pennant 1776, ii, p. 409, no. 12, built into Hoddom Castle near Birrens (cf. Wilson 1851, p. 397). However, it is now known to derive from Great Chesters fort (*Aesica*) on Hadrian's Wall; see bibliography at *RIB* 1747.

FALSA

(d) Tombstone

Birrens (*Blatobulgium*), Dumfriesshire.

An upright tombstone is known from a drawing by W. S. Irvine, in the margin of his *History of the Antiquities of Dumfriesshire* (MS formerly in the Library of the Society of Antiquaries of Scotland; not now traceable), which was copied by Daniel Wilson. See *CIL* vii 13*; *RIB* 2367*. The inscription is improbable and has long been judged to be a modern forgery. It should be noted that the stone is not specifically ascribed to Birrens by Irvine, but may have been copied into his MS only because of similarities in decorative motifs to the altar of Minerva (here no. 9), beside which it appears in Irvine's work.

(e) Tombstone of an Auxiliary Trooper

PLATE 42

Camelon, Stirlingshire.

An upright gravestone showing a cavalryman riding down an armed native warrior was found within the grounds of Camelon House in 1901, c.0.8 km south-east of the fort-site. T. Ross, *PSAS* xxxvi, 1901-2, pp. 606-10 with fig. 7; A. Gibb, *Scottish Antiquary* xvi, 1902, pp. 217-20 with figure. The slab was secured for the National Museum of Antiquities of Scotland. Modern opinion has been unanimous in dismissing it as a forgery of the later nineteenth century; see RCAHMS 1963, i, p. 111 n. 9; G. S. Maxwell, *PSAS* cii, 1969-70, pp. 285-7. It may have been intended as a garden ornament at Camelon House.

INDEXES

DEITIES

MILITARY UNITS

PERSONS

PLACES

PLATE 1

1 ($\frac{1}{8}$)

2 top ($\frac{1}{8}$)

2 left side ($\frac{1}{12}$)

2 front ($\frac{1}{12}$)

2 right side ($\frac{1}{12}$)

PLATE 2

3 ($\frac{1}{12}$)

4 (scale unknown)

5 ($\frac{1}{10}$)

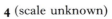

6 ($\frac{1}{5}$)

PLATE 3

7 $(\frac{1}{12})$

8 *left side* $(\frac{1}{10})$ 8 *front* $(\frac{1}{10})$ 8 *right side* $(\frac{1}{10})$

PLATE 4

9 *left side* ($\frac{1}{12}$)   9 *front* ($\frac{1}{12}$)   9 *right side* ($\frac{1}{12}$)   10 ($\frac{1}{4}$)

11 ($\frac{1}{4}$)

12 ($\frac{1}{10}$)

PLATE 5

13 ($\frac{1}{8}$)

14 ($\frac{1}{8}$)

15 ($\frac{1}{10}$)

15 *top* ($\frac{1}{5}$)

PLATE 6

16 ($\frac{1}{10}$)

17 *left side* ($\frac{1}{10}$)

17 *front* ($\frac{1}{10}$)

17 *right side* ($\frac{1}{10}$)

PLATE 7

18 $\left(\frac{3}{5}\right)$

20 $\left(\frac{2}{5}\right)$

21 $\left(\frac{1}{2}\right)$

PLATE 8

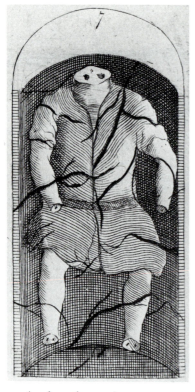

22 (scale unknown)

23 (scale unknown)

25 ($\frac{1}{10}$)

PLATE 9

26

26a ($\frac{1}{10}$)

26b ($\frac{1}{5}$)

26c ($\frac{1}{3}$)

26d ($\frac{1}{4}$)

PLATE 10

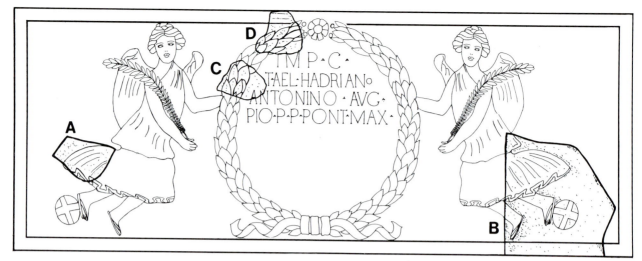

IMP·C·
T·AEL·HADRIAN·o
ANTONINO · AVG ·
PIO·P·P·PONT·MAX·

27

27a $(\frac{1}{4})$

27c $(\frac{1}{5})$

27b $(\frac{1}{5})$

27d $(\frac{1}{3})$

PLATE 11

28 $\left(\frac{1}{5}\right)$

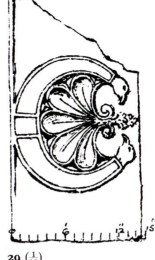

29 $\left(\frac{1}{10}\right)$

30a,b,c $\left(\frac{1}{5}\right)$

30d $\left(\frac{1}{3}\right)$

31 $\left(\frac{1}{4}\right)$

32 $\left(\frac{3}{4}\right)$

PLATE 12

33a $(\frac{1}{4})$

33b $(\frac{1}{2})$

33c $(\frac{2}{5})$

33d,e,f $(\frac{1}{2})$

33g $(\frac{1}{3})$

33h $(\frac{1}{4})$

PLATE 13

34a $\left(\frac{1}{4}\right)$

34b $\left(\frac{1}{4}\right)$

34c $\left(\frac{2}{5}\right)$

35 $\left(\frac{1}{3}\right)$

36a $\left(\frac{1}{3}\right)$

36b $\left(\frac{1}{5}\right)$

37a $\left(\frac{1}{3}\right)$

37b $\left(\frac{1}{3}\right)$

37c $\left(\frac{1}{3}\right)$

PLATE 14

38 $\left(\tfrac{1}{3}\right)$

39 $\left(\tfrac{1}{3}\right)$

40 $\left(\tfrac{1}{4}\right)$

41 $\left(\tfrac{1}{4}\right)$

43 $\left(\tfrac{1}{20}\right)$

42 $\left(\tfrac{1}{8}\right)$

PLATE 15

44 $(\frac{1}{4})$

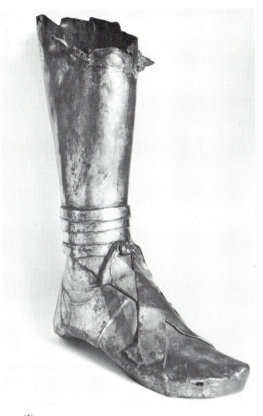

45 $(\frac{1}{6})$

46 *left side* $(\frac{1}{10})$ **46** *front* $(\frac{1}{10})$ **46** *right side* $(\frac{1}{10})$

PLATE 16

47 ($\frac{1}{12}$)

48 *left side* ($\frac{1}{12}$)

48 *front* ($\frac{1}{12}$)

48 *right side* ($\frac{1}{12}$)

49 ($\frac{1}{3}$)

50 ($\frac{1}{4}$)

PLATE 17

51 $(\frac{1}{5})$

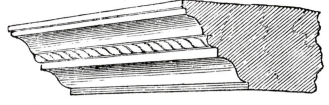

52 $(\frac{1}{8})$

53 $(\frac{1}{5})$

52 $(\frac{1}{2})$

54 *front* $(\frac{2}{5})$

54 *back* $(\frac{2}{5})$

PLATE 18

55 ($\frac{1}{2}$)

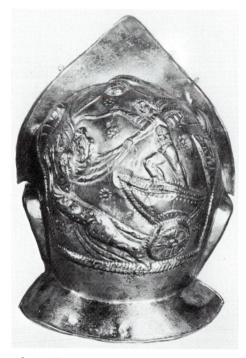

56 *top* ($\frac{1}{4}$)

56 *front* ($\frac{1}{4}$)

PLATE 19

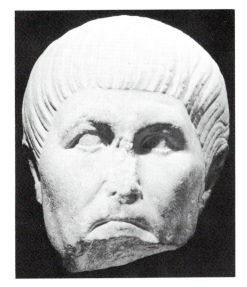

57 $(\frac{1}{4})$

58 $(\frac{1}{2})$

59 $(\frac{1}{12})$

60 $(\frac{1}{4})$

61 $(\frac{1}{10})$

PLATE 20

62 (scale unknown)

65

66 ($\frac{1}{12}$)

PLATE 21

67 (scale unknown)

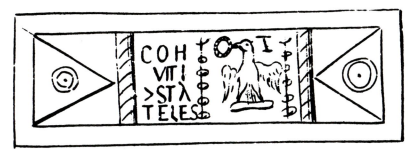

68 ($\frac{1}{20}$)

68 *left* ($\frac{1}{10}$)

68 *right* ($\frac{1}{10}$)

PLATE 22

69 $\left(\frac{1}{3}\right)$

70 $\left(\frac{1}{2}\right)$

71 $\left(\frac{1}{5}\right)$

72 $\left(\frac{1}{10}\right)$

73 $\left(\frac{1}{5}\right)$

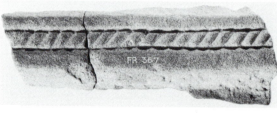

74 $\left(\frac{1}{2}\right)$

PLATE 23

75 ($\frac{1}{2}$)

76 ($\frac{1}{4}$)

77 ($\frac{1}{10}$)

78 ($\frac{1}{8}$)

79 ($\frac{1}{3}$)

80 ($\frac{1}{10}$)

PLATE 24

81 ($\frac{1}{5}$)

82 ($\frac{1}{10}$)

84 ($\frac{1}{10}$)

85 (scale unknown)

PLATE 25

86 *top* ($\frac{1}{5}$)

86 ($\frac{1}{8}$)

87 ($\frac{1}{10}$)

88a ($\frac{1}{5}$)

88b ($\frac{1}{8}$)

90 ($\frac{1}{5}$)

PLATE 26

91 ($\frac{1}{8}$)

92 *left side* ($\frac{1}{10}$) **92** *back* ($\frac{1}{10}$) **92** *front* ($\frac{1}{10}$) **92** *right side* ($\frac{1}{10}$)

PLATE 27

93 $\left(\frac{1}{3}\right)$

94 *front* $\left(\frac{1}{10}\right)$

94 *right side* $\left(\frac{1}{10}\right)$

95 (scale unknown)

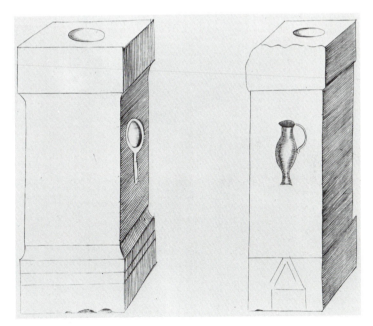

96 (scale unknown)

PLATE 28

97 $(\frac{1}{5})$

98 $(\frac{1}{5})$

99 $(\frac{1}{5})$

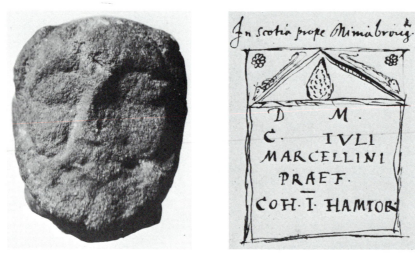

100 $(\frac{1}{2})$

101 (scale unknown)

102 $(\frac{1}{10})$

PLATE 29

103 $\left(\frac{1}{8}\right)$

104 $\left(\frac{1}{8}\right)$

105 $\left(\frac{1}{10}\right)$

106 $\left(\frac{1}{12}\right)$

107 $\left(\frac{1}{20}\right)$

108 $\left(\frac{1}{10}\right)$

PLATE 30

109 $(\frac{1}{8})$

111 $(\frac{1}{12})$

112 $(\frac{1}{12})$

110 $(\frac{1}{20})$

113 $(\frac{1}{12})$

PLATE 31

114 ($\frac{1}{12}$)

115 ($\frac{1}{10}$)

116 (scale unknown)

119 ($\frac{1}{4}$)

122 ($\frac{1}{20}$)

PLATE 32

123 $\left(\frac{1}{12}\right)$

124 (scale unknown)

125 $\left(\frac{1}{4}\right)$

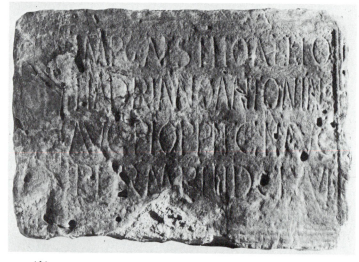

127 $\left(\frac{1}{10}\right)$

126 $\left(\frac{1}{3}\right)$

128 $\left(\frac{1}{10}\right)$

PLATE 33

129 $\left(\frac{1}{8}\right)$

130 $\left(\frac{1}{8}\right)$

131 $\left(\frac{1}{8}\right)$

132 $\left(\frac{1}{2}\right)$

133 $\left(\frac{1}{2}\right)$

134 $\left(\frac{1}{5}\right)$

PLATE 34

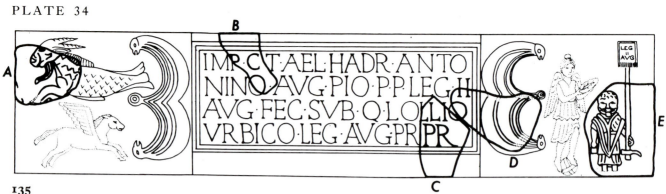

135

135a $(\frac{1}{8})$

135b $(\frac{1}{12})$

135c,d $(\frac{1}{20})$

135e $(\frac{1}{10})$

137 $(\frac{1}{12})$

PLATE 35

138 ($\frac{1}{12}$)

139 ($\frac{2}{5}$)

140 ($\frac{1}{4}$)

141 ($\frac{1}{2}$)

142 ($\frac{1}{2}$)

PLATE 36

143 ($\frac{1}{5}$)

145 ($\frac{1}{12}$)

146 ($\frac{1}{12}$)

148 ($\frac{1}{12}$)

147 ($\frac{1}{8}$)

PLATE 37

149 ($\frac{1}{10}$)

150 ($\frac{1}{12}$)

151 ($\frac{1}{8}$)

152 ($\frac{1}{10}$)

PLATE 38

153 *left* ($\frac{1}{10}$)

153 *right* ($\frac{1}{10}$)

154 ($\frac{1}{8}$)

155 ($\frac{1}{10}$)

156 ($\frac{1}{10}$)

157 ($\frac{1}{10}$)

PLATE 39

159 ($\frac{1}{8}$)

158 ($\frac{1}{12}$)

160 ($\frac{1}{5}$)

161 *front* ($\frac{1}{5}$)

161 *side* ($\frac{1}{5}$)

PLATE 40

162 $(\frac{1}{2})$

163 $(\frac{1}{3})$

164 $(\frac{2}{5})$

165 (scale unknown)

166 $(\frac{1}{2})$

PLATE 41

167 ($\frac{1}{4}$)

168 ($\frac{1}{3}$)

169 ($\frac{1}{3}$)

170 ($\frac{3}{4}$)

171 ($\frac{1}{12}$)

PLATE 42

172 $\left(\frac{1}{8}\right)$

falsa e